Bishop with a Pastor's Heart

Bishop with a
Pastor's
Heart

Kenneth W. Copeland

Thomas S. McAnally

*To Bishop McCleskey,
another bishop with a pastor's
heart—and a vision for
a better world.*

Thomas S. McAnally

Providence House Publishers

PROVIDENCE PUBLISHING CORPORATION
FRANKLIN, TENNESSEE

Printed in the United States of America

10   09   08   07   06   1   2   3   4   5

Library of Congress Control Number: 2006932860

ISBN-13: 978-1-57736-378-1
ISBN-10: 1-57736-378-7

Page design by Joey McNair
Cover design by LeAnna Massingille

PROVIDENCE HOUSE PUBLISHERS
an imprint of
Providence Publishing Corporation
238 Seaboard Lane • Franklin, Tennessee 37067
www.providence-publishing.com
800-321-5692

Contents

Foreword

In the endless line of splendor of Methodist bishops, the life of Kenneth W. Copeland is a unique witness to the transforming power of the Gospel of Jesus Christ. Tom McAnally has provided a clear picture of the distinctive features of this inspiring preacher, evangelist, and pastor. Those who read these pages will be as challenged as those who heard him preach and witnessed his earthly ministry.

Catherine Copeland has for many years wanted to produce a book that would reflect the life and ministry of her beloved husband. I encouraged her to pursue that vision, and I was honored when she asked me to write this foreword.

This book is a reminder of the mind-boggling changes in the twentieth century. The son of an itinerant Methodist pastor, Kenneth Copeland came to maturity in the midst of the Great Depression. He knew from personal experience how families with limited resources survived by sacrificing for one another.

He began preaching as a teenager, while the Church was riding the crest of enthusiasm that lingered from the missionary and evangelistic advances of the nineteenth century. As a young pastor, he knew the agonies produced by the horrors of war. He shared the vision for proud mergers which united different streams of Methodist heritage. In this period of rapid social change and remarkable advances in transportation, communication, and prosperity, he was dedicated to keeping the proclamation of the Gospel focused upon the good news for both personal and social salvation.

From memories of his father's preaching in the days of the horse-and-buggy to personal associations with astronauts who landed on the moon, he demonstrated the ability to translate the enduring message of the Gospel to the citizens of a constantly changing world.

My life has been enriched by a wide variety of associations with the Copeland family for more than six decades. Three months after the beginning of World War II, while I was yet in college, I was appointed as a student pastor to the Alba Circuit in the Tyler District in East Texas. John Wesley Copeland was serving his last appointment before retirement in the same district. Perhaps because we shared the same name—John Wesley—and also because he was the first Methodist Protestant clergyman I had known, we soon became warm friends. Later I learned that he had a son named Kenneth.

Three years later, I was appointed to Pleasant Retreat Church in Tyler. The Breedlove family in that congregation informed me that Kenneth and his family would be spending part of their vacation with them, and that he might be persuaded to preach for us on Sunday. That was the beginning of a lifetime friendship with Kenneth, Catherine, Pat, and Sue.

When a new sanctuary was opened in that Tyler church three years later, Kenneth came from Stillwater, Oklahoma, to preach the first revival. This began a tradition, as in later years Kenneth also preached the first revivals in new church buildings in the Texas communities of Atlanta and Beaumont.

We also became acquainted with three of Kenneth's brothers: Buck, when he lived in Corsicana; Bill, who came from Mt. Vernon to be our Layman's Day speaker in 1952; and Cleve, who was recognized on his ninetieth birthday at the Grand Avenue United Methodist Church in McAlester, Oklahoma, when I was visiting there.

FOREWORD

The large Copeland family nurtured close ties and often drove many miles to hear Kenneth preach. Several were present when he was consecrated as bishop at the 1960 South Central Jurisdictional Conference in San Antonio. Upon his election, I called our mutual friends in Tyler, Jesse and Leta Breedlove, who came for the consecration service.

Another high point of our relationship came in 1968, when Kenneth became our bishop in the Texas Conference. I had invited him to preach a revival in our new sanctuary in Beaumont before his election. Martha and I were unaware that, during that week, he had suggested to some of our members that they consider allowing us to visit Methodist mission work in other lands. A family made a designated gift to the church for that purpose, and later we spent an evening with Kenneth and Catherine in Houston. They outlined how such a trip might be organized, and how important such an experience might be.

Within a few weeks, we had engaged a travel agent, ordered our first passports, and developed a tentative schedule for a month-long trip around the world. We sent that proposal to Bishop Copeland, who wrote missionaries and Methodist leaders in Japan, Korea, Taiwan, Hong Kong, and India, encouraging them to help us see as much as possible. Our trip took place only a few days after American astronauts landed on the moon and was truly a life-changing experience.

Along with others in the Texas Conference, we were stunned by Bishop Copeland's untimely death. We have cherished opportunities to visit with Catherine and enjoyed sharing special memories of Kenneth with those who knew and loved him.

FOREWORD

The partnership which the Copelands shared was dedicated to ensuring that Kenneth might fully develop God's call upon his life. Catherine's total dedication to the publication of this book is a climax to that partnership. As their years were surrounded by many evidences of God's providence, so in that divine providence this book may allow other persons to discover or rekindle God's purpose for their lives.

In the more than three decades since Bishop Copeland entered the Church Triumphant, Catherine has continued to be engaged in the concerns of the United Methodist Church to which her husband contributed so much. Recognizing his devotion to the evangelistic mission of the church, she has given continuing leadership and inspiration to the United Methodist Foundation for Evangelism. Honoring that legacy, the spirit of evangelism will, I hope, be renewed from generation to generation as the witness of Kenneth Copeland is shared by those who read this book.

Whatever challenges the future may hold, the good news of the Gospel of Jesus Christ will continue to bring the fullness of joyful salvation to those whose lives are blessed by learning how Kenneth Copeland responded to God's call to proclaim that Good News.

John Wesley Hardt

Preface

Kenneth W. Copeland's life and ministry intersected with significant events in the history of both Methodism and the United States. He encouraged the poor and hungry during the Great Depression; preached racial equality during the civil rights movement of the 1950s and 1960s; spoke out against Communism and nuclear proliferation during the cold war; and called for peace and reconciliation during the Vietnam era. He applauded strides toward Christian unity represented by the Second Vatican Council; experienced, on a firsthand basis, the beginnings of the space age; and traveled the globe as an ambassador for Christ.

Kenneth led his small Methodist Protestant Church conference into the 1939 union, joining that denomination with two larger Methodist bodies that had split nearly a century earlier. His gift as a public speaker and his call to preach came early in life, propelling him to the pulpit of one of the largest congregations in Methodism and then, at age forty-eight, to the highest office of bishop.

His appointment as the episcopal leader of the Nebraska Area allowed him to become directly acquainted with the Evangelical United Brethren Church, which merged in 1968 with the Methodist Church to form the United Methodist Church. His commitment to racial equality and his nature as a reconciler were evident when black and white conferences merged in both the Nebraska and Houston areas.

PREFACE

Described as a man of persuasion, Kenneth Copeland's chief passions were evangelism and preaching. He considered no concern, issue, or topic off limits for the Christian faith.

His influence was felt far beyond Texas and Oklahoma, where he served as a local church pastor, and the Nebraska and Houston areas, where he was bishop. A world citizen, he was deeply involved in churchwide programs of mission, evangelism, education, disaster relief, new church development, and family life.

The Bishop was a husband and father whose definition of family was not limited to his own wife and daughters, but to brothers and sisters around the globe. He was a proponent for the support of church-related institutions such as colleges and hospitals, and a vocal opponent of the sale and use of alcoholic beverages.

Above all, Kenneth Copeland preached and lived Christ. More impressive than the profundity of his spoken messages was the example of a life lived in harmony with the call of Christ. His time on earth ended at age sixty-one, while still in active service as a bishop in Houston. Premature was the word used by many at the time of his death. However, as one colleague observed, "Kenneth Copeland did more for the cause of Christianity in five years than most people do in fifteen."

It was my privilege to serve as director of communications for the Nebraska Annual Conference for almost six years during Bishop Copeland's service in the Cornhusker State in the late 1960s. Like so many of

PREFACE

his colleagues and friends, my life has been blessed by his authentic Christian witness. He walked the talk. He lived what he preached. He was on the street what he was in the pulpit.

I was honored when Mrs. Copeland asked me to record something about this faithful servant. The credit for this book belongs to her. She had the vision and provided essential details through hours of interviews.

For those who knew Bishop Copeland, I hope I have included the most significant aspects of his life. For those who didn't, I hope you find in these pages inspiration for your own faith journey.

Acknowledgments

S pecial thanks to the many friends and associates who shared their memories of Bishop Copeland; to his wife, Catherine, and their daughters, Patti and Sue, for their personal and detailed recollections; to Page A. Thomas and his staff at the Center for Methodist Studies at Bridwell Library in Dallas, Texas, where the Copeland papers are located; to John Wesley Hardt, Bishop-in-Residence Emeritus at Perkins School of Theology, and an enthusiastic advocate for the preservation of Methodist history; and to Mrs. Virgil Lundell and Debbie Dial for their loving support.

1

The Early Years

Throughout Christian history, individuals from humble beginnings have responded to the call of God upon their lives and accomplished great things. Such was the case for Kenneth Wilford Copeland, born April 3, 1912, in the Ozark Mountain region of north Arkansas.

One might have predicted that this infant, born in a Methodist parsonage to a father named for Methodism's founder, John Wesley, would be destined for a life of Christian service. Kenneth was the sixth of ten children born to John Wesley and Nancy (Hively) Copeland, married October 1, 1896. His parents had eight boys and two girls: Cleve, Pearl, Esther, Otto, Alvin "Buck," Kenneth, Kennard "Bill," Albert (who died as an infant), Ray, and John Wesley Jr.

Kenneth entered the world in the year that Woodrow Wilson was elected president, New Mexico was admitted to the Union, and the Girl Scouts of America was founded by Juliette Gordon Low. A week after his birth, the "unsinkable" ocean liner *RMS Titanic* left port from Southampton, England, on its ill-fated maiden voyage. The country was on the doorstep of World War I. Among notable people sharing his birth year were chef Julia Child, actress and singer Dale Evans, musician Woody Guthrie, and presidential spouse Lady Bird Johnson.

Kenneth's father, a farmer, served as a supply pastor in the Batesville, Arkansas District of the White River Annual Conference of the Methodist Episcopal Church South. His appointments included Pleasant Plains (1906), Wolf Bayou (1907–08), Mountain View Circuit (1909), Bexar Circuit (1910–13), Desha Circuit (1914), Calico Rock Circuit (1915), and Norfork Circuit (1916). He was serving the Bexar Circuit in Fulton County, bordering Missouri, when Kenneth was born.

It is not known why his parents chose Kenneth as their son's first name, but Wilford was chosen to honor Boone L. Wilford, presiding elder of the Batesville District. According to Arkansas historian Vester Williams, the presiding elder came to visit the parsonage family and was asked to baptize the new infant. In an October 20, 1966, article in the *Salem Headlight* newspaper, Williams observed that Wilford had no idea he was baptizing a baby who would become one of America's greatest preachers and a widely known personality listed in *Who's Who in America*.

The infant Kenneth and his siblings soon joined their father as he traveled by horse-drawn buggy to preaching appointments, some of which were twenty miles from home. A few years after Kenneth's birth, the Copeland family moved to a cotton farm at Midlothian, near

Chandler in Lincoln County, Oklahoma, where they farmed and where John Wesley continued to preach.

Unquestionably, the greatest influence in Kenneth's early life was his father. In a 1951 Father's Day sermon, Kenneth said his father exhibited the "face and faith of one who knows the mastery of life." He told of living in Oklahoma, where tornadoes and storms regularly ravaged the state.

> We always had a storm cellar by the side of the house. It was a part of the equipment of life. Every time a serious cloud would come up in the night, my father would arouse the sleeping children from their beds at two or three o'clock in the morning and lead us to the cellar. There we sat, half-asleep until the danger was past.
>
> It was hard for a young child to fully appreciate the meaning of these moments. I shall never forget, however, the role my father played in this tense drama. He was the last one in. He would sit on the steps or stand outside as long as possible, watching and waiting. I see him now, as he stood silhouetted against the background of the dark and foreboding clouds, the wise interpreter of danger. But more than that, he stood between his loved ones and danger to protect us with his life. Small in stature though he was, he was strong and courageous and was, for me, the symbol of an everlasting mastery of life in times of stress and storm. It is impossible for me to properly evaluate the courage and inspiration he brought to my life in those early years.

By present-day standards, Kenneth's father was uneducated, completing only the fourth or fifth grade. His education as a preacher was even less impressive:

no college training, no seminars, no retreats, no study groups, no course of study, nothing that marks the educational preparation of preachers today. He did not own an encyclopedia, reference book, or commentary. His reference library was his Bible.

John Wesley Copeland professed Christianity and answered God's call to preach after he was married. "He picked up his Bible and started preaching," said his son Bill. "He was dynamic in the pulpit, moving from one side to the other with his Bible in his hand. His study was wherever he found a quiet place from his family and talkative wife: in the barn lot, on a log in the pasture, or in the bedroom, always with his Bible in his hand."

Nancy was devout and expressive in her faith. Bill described her as a "shoutin' Methodist" who made no effort to restrain her enthusiasm for the faith.

Despite the difficulties of everyday life, the Copeland family found joy in each other and in music. All family members, particularly Buck and Cleve, were singers and fans of gospel music, but it was acknowledged among siblings that Kenneth was the most musically talented.

Bill recalls the family singing on the telephone when they lived in Oklahoma. "We were on a party line. After someone called and asked us to sing, they would give five long rings, which really meant 'emergency,' and announce, 'The Copeland family is going to sing for us.' We would all gather close to the telephone and sing gospel songs. We all sang for most of our lives. None was a really accomplished singer, but we always pitched in." The entire family also kept the farm operating efficiently and productively. The primary crops were cotton and alfalfa hay.

When neighboring children came to visit, a worship service was often a part of the play activity. Kenneth, standing on a bench or chair, was always the preacher. "With real sincerity I would make a passionate plea for the members of my congregation to accept Christ as Savior," he wrote years later in a book titled *My Call to Preach*. He told of preaching sermons while walking down a winding pasture lane bringing the cows home in the evening. When he and his brothers would pause to rest from picking cotton, Kenneth would seize the opportunity and preach.

Kenneth's brother Ray also followed in the footsteps of their father and became a Methodist minister. Kennard, known as Bill, was born two years after Kenneth. Of all the siblings, a special bond existed between these two. Bill's son Kenneth Claud, a medical doctor on staff at the University of Oklahoma Medical School in Oklahoma City, is named for his uncle.

When their father had health difficulties, the family quit farming and sold their farm machinery and live-stock. When John Wesley's health improved, they rented a farm near Chandler and resumed sharecropping.

"We got in our crops there and it was nearly time for cotton picking when Dad got the call to go to Sparks as pastor," Bill recalled. "He was eager to accept the assignment, but the crops had to be harvested. It was also time for school to start. Buck, Otto, and I remained on the farm to pick the cotton, and Dad, Mom, J. W., and Kenneth moved to Sparks."

It was at Sparks that fourteen-year-old Kenneth felt the call to preach, an experience he later described as being both gradual and sudden. "From my earliest recollection I had a burning desire to preach," he wrote. "The fact that I was born in a Methodist parsonage and reared in a minister's home might account for much of that desire. Certainly I shall be eternally grateful for this home background and for the spiritual atmosphere my father and mother threw around me in those early days."

He remembers that at the age of twelve, "In simple childlike faith I accepted Christ as my Savior, kneeling at an altar under a brush arbor beside a small country church, about three miles east of Chandler, Oklahoma." Two years later, while spending a few weeks with his oldest brother and helping with farm work, he experienced, "the deepest stirrings of the human heart I had ever known. I was driven to frequent prayers and tears and to the sincerest searchings of my spirit. I had never been so moved in all my life; something was surely taking place within me. When I returned home, I was still troubled and continued to pray earnestly."

A few weeks later, he went with his father and mother to revival services held at a church of another denomination in Sparks.

> I remember neither the evangelist's name nor the sermon that night. While I sat there with my parents in that spiritual atmosphere, however, there came to my heart the clearest possible revelation that God had laid his hand upon me and wanted me to preach his glorious Gospel. Since that night, I have had no desire or occasion to doubt the fact that the still small voice of God, speaking

spirit with spirit in a clear, positive, unmistakable language, showed me his will for my life.

He recalled his parents being supremely happy when learning of his experience. They had always wanted him to become a minister, but intentionally had not asked him or pushed him. "They wanted the call, if there was to be one, to come from God and not from men," wrote Kenneth. "For this I shall always be grateful to them."

In addition to being both gradual and sudden, the call to preach for Kenneth was a continuing revelation. "It is not simply a memory," he wrote. "It is not simply the finding of a light once. It was not simply written orders delivered once and filed away for future reference. It continues to abide with me in an ever-growing revelation. I think I know what Paul meant when he said, 'Woe is me, if I preach not the Gospel.'"

Kenneth preached his first sermon before a "real" congregation in the summer of 1926. His father, speaking at a series of revival meetings under a brush arbor in Warwick, Oklahoma, announced to those gathered that Kenneth, age fourteen, would preach the next night. Later in his life, he recalled that first sermon, which was based on the parable of the Prodigal Son:

> There sat my father behind me to give adequate and full support to his young son. Of course he gave me a generous flow of Methodist "amens." These meant a great deal to me then, more than I can tell you, and they would still mean a great deal to me now. . . . But even more than this, as I stood there trying to deliver my soul, I felt that here behind me was one who had learned the mastery of

the ministry as no other man in my acquaintance had learned it.

Certainly no bishop could have meant as much to me then as my father meant. No preacher who ever lived inspired me like he did. I saw in him a Christian mastery of life and felt in his love for me the security of life. When my youthful spirit would unwisely run to some extreme and I would then sense its danger, I had only to seek the shelter of my father's bosom and there in his brave courageous heart find the support and strength I needed for the facing of that particular hour.

At fifteen, Kenneth was denied a license to preach because of his young age.

I left that district conference a disappointed lad. The memory is as fresh as the morning newspaper. Beside me walked my father. He neither condemned nor justified the action of the committee. His only word was this: "Son, as long as I have a pulpit, you can preach in it." When he said that, I cared little at the moment whether I had a license or not. Why should I worry? I had just been licensed by the greatest preacher that ever lived—my father.

All my life his hands have been laid on me and now he gave me further assurance that his pulpit would always be open to me. What other authority could I ask for? He has always symbolized for me, in his quiet but dynamic spirit, the victory that overcometh the world, and I want to honor him today with the sincerest love of the grateful heart of a son. My greatest desire finds fulfillment in the anticipation that I might become the kind of son he has always wanted me to be. May my dear Heavenly Father grant me the wisdom and the courage to achieve this coveted goal.

THE EARLY YEARS

In the fall of 1927, Kenneth's father was assigned to a church in Wellston, Oklahoma. While there, Bill and Kenneth joined other school children for a train trip to the state fair in Oklahoma City. A highlight of the trip was seeing Charles Lindbergh wave from the *Spirit of St. Louis* as he flew low over the fairgrounds. While in Oklahoma City, Lindbergh spoke to thousands at Methodist-related Oklahoma City University.

At Wellston, the family purchased its first car, a Model T Ford. Movies became popular during this period, but the Copeland children were allowed to see only a few that were approved by their father.

In 1928, the family switched its membership from the Methodist Episcopal Church South to the Methodist Protestant Church, a decision that would greatly influence Kenneth in later years. (The family remained in the Methodist Protestant Church until church union in 1939.) The denomination had been formed in 1830 as the result of differences on several issues by a sizable group in the Methodist Episcopal Church. The key issues at dispute were the role of bishops, the desire to elect the presiding elders, and approval for lay persons to be voting members of the annual conferences. The new denomination held its first General Conference in 1834. It had no bishops.

Pastor Copeland accepted an invitation to serve the Methodist Protestant Church at Quinton, approximately thirty miles northeast of McAlester. The building there was constructed of bricks, a first for the Copeland family.

By that time, sixteen-year-old Kenneth had already developed a reputation as an outstanding preacher. He

9

preached occasionally in Quinton for his dad and served part-time at a nearby, small, country church. While in Quinton, the young people of the church produced a three-act play titled *Deacon Dubbs* that was, according to Bill, a real hit in the community. Because of the reputation he had already gained as a young preacher, Kenneth had the lead role.

During the summer of 1929, Buck and Kenneth traveled to Texas with their father for a series of revival meetings. Because of contacts made there, their father was invited to relocate to the Texas Conference. The family moved to Wortham, Texas, in midsummer to wait for an appointment at the annual conference session in the fall. Kenneth and Bill attended school in Wortham for six weeks before their father was assigned to Corsicana.

Corsicana was the first large community for the Copeland family. The church was a small, white-frame building across the street from the high school. The congregation included few young people when the Copelands arrived, but Kenneth's dynamic personality and his preaching attracted others. "Kenneth held the group together," recalled Bill. "If some activity was questioned in any way, it would not be, 'What will our parents say?' but 'What will Kenneth say?'"

As a high school student, Kenneth developed an impressive vocabulary and enjoyed language studies. After his two older sisters married and left home, the duties on the farm, including household chores, were left to the boys. Kenneth and Bill would practice sentence structure from an open textbook on the kitchen table while washing dishes after dinner each evening. "I'm sure I learned more grammar from him than I did any teacher," Bill said.

The *Corsican* yearbook, published during Kenneth's senior year in 1930, reported that he was among students receiving *As* every six weeks. More revealing was a statement about his speaking abilities: "In extemporaneous speaking, Kenneth Copeland won first place easily. Kenneth is a polished orator." That would remain an accurate description throughout his life.

Kenneth was invited to preach at a citywide revival meeting involving most of the churches in Corsicana. At the invitation of his teachers and classmates, he preached the baccalaureate sermon at his own graduation. His topic was "The Supreme Court of Moral Appeals."

The stock market crashed on Black Thursday, October 24, 1929, ushering in the Great Depression. Large numbers of people lived in poverty, desperately in need of more food, clothing, and shelter. It was against this backdrop that Kenneth, with a high school diploma in hand, enrolled at Westminster College in Tehuacana, Texas.

Westminster was established near McKinney, Texas, by Methodist Protestants in 1895, with two teachers and a two-story frame building. In 1897, it was reorganized as a four-year college and granted a state charter. The school moved to Tehuacana in 1902.

Westminster was only thirty miles from Corsicana, so Kenneth spent weekdays on campus and returned home each weekend. Bill and other young people piled into the family's Model A Ford each Sunday evening to take Kenneth back to school.

Bill recalled an incident during one of those trips that illustrates Kenneth's early moral character.

> As we were leaving Corsicana, we stopped at a filling station for gasoline. Stalks of bananas hung between the driveways. I was sitting on the passenger side of the front seat with my arm resting on an open window. My arm extended out of the window and my hand fell upon a banana on the stalk; my fingers closed on it. Kenneth drove off, and the banana pulled off the stalk. As we started down the road, I calmly started peeling the banana. I made some smart-aleck comment that it came off in my hand. Kenneth quickly turned the car around and drove back to the station and said, "Now go in and pay for the banana." I paid, and I am sure that no more bananas have fallen off into my hands since then.

Kenneth was ordained an elder in the Methodist Protestant Church in 1931, at the age of nineteen. He served for one year as his father's associate at Corsicana, and graduated from Westminster in 1932. That fall he was appointed to his own congregation in Cooper, and his father was assigned to a five-point circuit with residence in Slocum.

Kenneth initially shared the parsonage in Cooper with a family that provided free meals in return for their rent. He supplemented his small salary by working Saturdays at a local shoe store, making enough money to continue his education at East Texas State Teacher's College in Commerce, Texas.

2

My Catherine

During his appointment in Cooper, Kenneth and his father were invited to preach a summer revival at a Methodist Protestant Church in San Angelo.

A few days before the meeting began, Maxine, the young daughter of brother Cleve and his wife, Jenny, became ill with pneumonia and died. Kenneth traveled to San Angelo to start the revival, while his dad and Bill went to Chandler, Oklahoma, to be with Cleve and the family. After the funeral, the two headed for San Angelo, but were delayed for two days just south of the Texas-Oklahoma border with car trouble. Meanwhile, the revival meeting was well underway with Kenneth in the pulpit.

Catherine Andrews was a student at Daniel Baker University in Brownwood, Texas. Her family had moved to San Angelo after her father's furniture business in Brownwood collapsed during the Depression. In order to return to Daniel Baker in the fall, Catherine took a summer job working at the soda fountain in the local F. W. Woolworth store.

A friend of the family encouraged Catherine's parents to "come hear this good little preacher out on North Chadbourne Street." Catherine and her mother accepted the invitation and, after the service, were introduced to the young evangelist.

Two days later, Kenneth came to the soda fountain and told Catherine he had missed her at services the previous night. With a nod, she quickly explained that if he was going to continue sitting at the counter, he would have to purchase something or she would lose her job. He complied with the store rules, but before leaving, had a commitment from Catherine that she would attend services that night and allow him to take her home afterward. Later in his ministry he was described as a man of persuasion, a character trait he obviously possessed as a young suitor.

Before the summer revival ended, the two agreed to correspond. A flurry of letters immediately began between San Angelo and Cooper, catching the attention of the mailman, a member of Kenneth's church. By extension, many in the small congregation soon learned of the budding romance.

Before leaving San Angelo, Kenneth assured Catherine that he would return for a visit, even though the Depression made travel financially difficult. And return he did, with a proposal of marriage. "I was shocked," she recalled. "When he took me home that night, he wanted to go in and talk with my father about our marriage, but I prevented that. The next day I talked to Mother, who in turn talked with Daddy. That prepared the way for Kenneth's visit the next

Sunday. There was this smile from Daddy, like he didn't want to admit it was okay, but it was."

Kenneth returned to San Angelo for one other visit before the two were married on October 5, 1933. Catherine was a member of the First Methodist Episcopal Church South in San Angelo, but the wedding was held at the little frame church on North Chadbourne where Kenneth had led revival services and where the two first met. Kenneth's father performed the ceremony. Kenneth was twenty-one; Catherine, eighteen.

Catherine did not return to school, choosing instead the role of a preacher's wife. Throughout their life together, Kenneth affectionately called her "my Catherine."

"It is humorous now to look back on the financial limitations we had in those early appointments," Catherine said. "Kenneth had two white shirts. I was always washing and ironing one shirt while he was wearing the other. Following a church service, a friend who knew of this shirt situation came up to Kenneth, touched his shirt collar lightly, and quipped, 'I just wanted to see if it was still hot!'"

Catherine was also deeply moved by the commitment of members who, despite the Depression, still found resources to support the church. One Saturday morning while Kenneth was working at the shoe store, Catherine answered a knock at the parsonage. There stood an elderly member who explained that she had sold a chicken in order to give money for the church. In her outstretched hand the woman presented fifty cents. "It brought tears to my eyes, and I will never forget it," said Catherine.

She and Kenneth learned much about life from church members who were frequent visitors in their home. It was clear from those early years that the two had a team ministry. "Kenneth made me feel so needed to the ministry that I never felt put upon," said Catherine.

In his first months at Cooper, Kenneth participated in gospel music events. He often preached Sunday morning, attended singing conventions in the afternoon, and returned to preach again Sunday night. Kenneth played the piano, organ, guitar, violin, and harmonica, and sang with a popular men's quartet. As family and church responsibilities increased, the quartet disbanded and he attended musical events less frequently.

Their first child, Patricia "Patti" Ann, was born at home on September 26, 1934. Finances became so tight that they sold their automobile. Soon after Patti's birth, Kenneth was appointed to the First Methodist Protestant Church in South Dallas, a new congregation of about one hundred members. The salary was sixty dollars a month, and no parsonage was provided. The church building had only subflooring, and the walls were lined only with cardboard that had been donated by a local funeral parlor.

When the offering was taken during worship services each Sunday night, the treasurer would drop the money in Kenneth's pocket. After breakfast the next morning, Kenneth would count the money and set aside a tenth. "We always gave a tithe, no matter what the salary," said Catherine.

Even though money was tight, Kenneth took classes at Southern Methodist University from the fall of 1936 to the spring of 1938, majoring in English. To reach the campus each day, he took at least two different city buses and a streetcar. He returned home for lunch and spent most afternoons visiting church members.

He was awarded his bachelor of arts degree on June 7, 1938. Twenty-six years later, on June 1, 1964, SMU awarded Copeland, then a bishop, an honorary doctor of laws degree. At the presentation, Professor Douglas Ewing Jackson described Copeland as "eloquent in the pulpit and constructive in administration."

A second daughter, Martha Sue, was born to the Copelands at Baylor Hospital in Dallas, on September 7, 1937. A devoted father, Kenneth declared, "How wondrously divine is the experience of uniting with God in the creative purpose of bringing a new life into the world. In this experience two loving hearts become one, not only with each other, but in a very real sense they become one with God. . . . Nothing can ever come to a husband and wife that could in any way take the place of a child."

As an adult, Patti recalled her sister saying, "I'm sorry you didn't have the kind of relationship with Daddy that I had." Patti said, "I laughed because I had that same feeling all my life. I felt sorry that Sue didn't have the kind or relationship with Daddy I had. That's how special he was to each of us. He made each of us feel special."

Catherine said the children learned early that church crises could change family plans. "But plans were always postponed, not canceled," she said.

Years later Kenneth preached a sermon titled "One Plus One Equals One," in which he paid tribute to Catherine.

She, more than anyone else, has sought to make our home a temple at whose altar the family has had the supreme joy of bringing every success and failure, every defeat and victory, every sorrow and joy and there shared them in the presence of him who both sanctifies and blesses the home. How she has been able to love me in spite of my weaknesses, work with me in spite of my limitations, and share my labors in spite of the excessive amount I have laid on her shoulders remains a mystery which I gladly accept and will not endeavor to solve.

Kenneth's characteristic humor was evident in the sermon as he told of a woman who was asked, "Do you believe in clubs for men?" The woman responded, "No, not until you've tried kindness first."

Kenneth expressed concern for the changing roles that were taking place regarding family life and child rearing. "While I firmly believe in the value of community life and what the community might contribute to the home, nonetheless I deplore the trend all too often found that seeks to turn over to the community everything the home is supposed to do for family life. If the home life is destroyed, the destruction of the community life will inevitably and shortly follow."

The Copeland home always welcomed visitors, some of whom stayed weeks and even months. Lamar Cooper, Kenneth's closest friend, lived with the Copeland family in their three-room parsonage in Dallas for at least six months. "Coop" often took care of Sue and Patti when their parents had commitments outside the home.

A Methodist Protestant who shared Kenneth's love of music, Cooper gave up his dream of a career as a concert pianist to answer God's call to ministry. He was admitted on trial in the Texas Conference of the Methodist Protestant Church in 1934, the year the Copelands went to Dallas, and was ordained an elder in 1938. He received his associate degree in 1936 from Westminster College, and returned to teach English there from 1938 to 1941. He later earned two bachelor of arts degrees, a master of arts degree, and a doctor of philosophy degree. He served as a local church pastor and air force chaplain.

When Kenneth later became pastor of First Methodist Church in Stillwater, Oklahoma, he was influential in having Cooper appointed as the Wesley Foundation director at Oklahoma A&M, a position he held from 1946 to 1950.

From 1952 to 1976, Cooper was a counselor to students and a professor of Christian social ethics and Methodist studies at Perkins School of Theology at Southern Methodist University in Dallas. While there, he played a significant role in the desegregation of the SMU student body, which began with the enrollment of five black students at Perkins in September 1952.

Recognizing there would be some problems related to having the first black students on campus, Dean Merrimon Cuninggim met with the five students soon after their arrival and established a process of mutual consultation. He promised to be understanding and to give personal advice, and asked the students to promise they would share questions and concerns. They agreed, and he became the students' primary contact during the first year.

When Cooper joined the faculty, he assumed that role, doing a careful, sensitive, excellent job, according to Cuninggim. "This was important, for when some folks became critical, the factor that was most highly offensive turned out to be the policy of consultation whereby the Negroes were deciding some things for themselves."

Cooper died on May 17, 2001, in Dallas, and was buried in Kenneth's robe, given to him by the family after Bishop Copeland's death in 1973.

3

Methodist Union

After four years at the Dallas church, Kenneth was elected president of the Texas Conference of the Methodist Protestant Church in 1938. The family moved into the president's residence in Mexia, knowing that his job would soon end with the upcoming union of the Methodist Protestant, Methodist Episcopal, and Methodist Episcopal South churches.

During his one-year presidency, he played a significant role in helping Methodist Protestants move with confidence into the union and representing their history, concerns, and interests to the larger Methodist family. He also wrote a chapter on the history of "The Methodist Protestant Church in Texas" for a 1969 book, *History of Texas Methodism 1900–1960,* edited by Olin W. Nail. A portion of that chapter reads:

> The Protestant Methodism began in the early 1820s, when some clergy and lay members became dissatisfied with the rules of governance of the Methodist Episcopal

Church that excluded lay people from decision-making bodies. Articles were published advocating the "mutual rights of ministers and laymen" and the agitation for a more democratic form of government grew across the years. In 1828 the final break came with the Methodist Episcopal Church over these differences and a small band of ministers and laymen set about to perfect a new organization. By 1830, the organization was complete and was named the Methodist Protestant Church.

The primary issue was equal representation of laymen with ministers in the decision-making bodies of the church, Kenneth wrote. Protests against the episcopacy were secondary. The Methodist Protestant Church never had basic differences in theology with its historical Methodist heritage, he stressed.

Methodist Protestants had established mission churches in North Texas as early as 1829. In 1845, a Louisiana Conference was organized, which included the work in Texas. In 1848, the Methodist Protestants in the state were organized into a Texas Conference.

Early calls for union with the two larger Methodist denominations were not met with enthusiasm by Methodist Protestants in Texas, but as time went on, members became more reconciled with the movement. The plan was favored by the 1936 Texas Annual Conference with little opposition.

The conference uniting the three denominations was held in Kansas City in 1939. J. A. Richardson was the official Methodist Protestant delegate from the Texas Conference. Kenneth Copeland, the new president, was an alternate delegate. In his last president's message to the Texas Annual Conference, Kenneth said:

> This conference session not only closes another chapter in the history of a great church; it closes the book. This is the finale to an illustrious volume. Our emotions are easily stirred as we reminisce in the history of our beloved church. However, we close this book only to begin another still larger and, we trust, even more complete. Let us begin our manuscript with prayer and with caution. Yes, we take our hats off to the past, but we take our coats off to the future.

Members of the Methodist Episcopal Church South in Texas experienced only minor changes after the union, according to author Walter Vernon, in his book, *The Methodist Excitement in Texas.* "Although several changes in terminology had to be learned, the basic institutions remained much the same . . . Any feelings of anxiety apparently were experienced primarily by the former Northern Methodists and Methodist Protestants . . . As the final minutes of these conferences in 1939 show, their leaders sought to assuage their fears."

In Texas—from a broad perspective, at least—it was a case of a large majority absorbing two smaller minorities, Vernon wrote. Black Methodists, instead of being merged, were segregated into the Central Jurisdiction. Relationships between Methodist Protestants and Southern Methodists were never hostile, as they were between the two episcopal Methodisms, he noted.

The Methodist Protestant Conference in Texas was divided among four conferences in the state. Copeland was one of fifteen Methodist Protestant clergymen transferred into the North Texas Conference. Statewide, the Methodist Protestants contributed to the union fifty-one pastors, nine licensed preachers, 3,419 members, forty-two church buildings (valued at $96,850), nineteen parsonages (valued at $23,050), and Westminster College.

The Methodist Protestant Church had no bishops, but under the provisions of the plan of union, the delegates from that church met separately at Kansas City and elected John C. Broomfield and James H. Straughn to the episcopacy. Bishop Broomfield was assigned to the St. Louis Area of the South Central Jurisdiction, and Bishop Straughn was assigned to special service within the United States for one year to help Methodist Protestants adjust to life in the new church. In 1940 he was assigned to the Pittsburgh Area.

The final annual conference of the Texas Conference of the Methodist Protestant Church was held at Westminster College in October 1939. Bishop Broomfield, a former president of the Methodist Protestant General Conference, was present to assist Kenneth in completing the business of the conference and leading the body into the larger fellowship.

The most distinct contribution made by the Methodist Protestant Church to union was its form of organization, granting equal representation to ministers and laymen in the general, jurisdictional, and annual conferences. While these changes in administrative organization were significant, Kenneth once wrote that the spiritual contributions were of greater importance. "A fervent evangelism, a great heart-warming Gospel, true to the fundamental doctrines of the Methodist Church and to New Testament teaching, and a closely knit spiritual brotherhood characterized this small, but vitally alive church. This spirit found its way into the larger Methodist Church. . . ."

A photograph featured in many Methodist history books shows three men joining hands on the closing night of the uniting conference: Bishop John M. Moore of the Methodist Episcopal Church South, Bishop James H. Straughn of the Methodist Protestant Church, and Bishop Edwin H. Hughes of the Methodist Episcopal Church.

Straughn was among some Methodist Protestants who had difficulty adjusting to the union. Bishop Roy H. Short wrote in *History of the Council of Bishops of the United Methodist Church: 1939–1979*:

> There were no guarantees for the merging denomina-
> tions in Methodist union as there were for the first twelve
> years of the Methodist-Evangelical United Brethren union
> [in 1968]. Bishop Straughn soon began to fear that the
> Methodist Protestant group was just about to sink without
> a trace into the larger Methodist Church. He felt this more
> as time went on . . . He maintained, however, his loyalty
> to the church for whose union he had labored even when
> he was not too happy with what might be occurring.

An Unexpected Appointment

Meanwhile, Kenneth had been a consistent advo-cate for union. In his address at the last Methodist

Protestant Texas Conference, he urged the pastors to "make no unnecessary demands, but be subject to the appointing powers of the church." He also urged them to "be patient if our appointments do not meet with our expectations and desires."

Kenneth quickly learned how difficult it would be to follow that advice. He had been led to believe that he would receive a comparable appointment, possibly in the Dallas area, when his position as president of the Methodist Protestant Conference ended.

At the first meeting of the new North Texas Annual Conference in 1939, however, the Copelands waited for Kenneth's name to be read from the list of pastoral appointments. Clergy, particularly those serving small churches, did not know where they were being appointed until all assignments were read by the bishop at the close of the conference.

Appointments to the Dallas District were read, but Kenneth's name was not called. District after district, appointments were announced but still his name was absent. Finally, the bishop announced Kenneth's assignment: the Scotland Methodist Church in Wichita Falls. The former president of a conference found himself assigned to a small church with an annual salary of one thousand dollars. Knowing of their limited financial resources, a friend offered one hundred dollars, which Kenneth took as a loan in order to pay moving expenses for his family.

It was never clear why he received this appointment in the new denomination. It may have been that ministers in the small denomination were not known by the

leadership in the two larger bodies. In his disappoint-
ment, Kenneth turned to his good friend and mentor,
W. Angie Smith, for counsel. The two had become close
friends in Dallas, when Kenneth was pastor of the
Methodist Protestant Church, and Smith (who would
later be elected bishop) was pastor of downtown First
Methodist Episcopal Church South. Smith advised his
young protégé not to appeal or protest his first assignment in the new denomination. He urged Kenneth to
go, do a good job, and expect a better appointment in
the future. That proved to be the case. Kenneth served
in Wichita Falls only one year.

Even though his tenure in that church was brief,
Kenneth's abilities were quickly recognized in the
community. A local radio station gave him time for a
weekly thirty-minute radio program, and school officials invited him to preach the baccalaureate service
for graduating seniors. He also served during this time
as a delegate to the first conference of the newly
created South Central Jurisdiction, an eight-state entity
that stretched from Nebraska to Louisiana. The 1940
jurisdictional conference was held in Oklahoma City.

Moving to Wichita Falls was a big adjustment for
the Copelands. Throughout her life, Catherine was
known for her chin-up attitude, but the new assignment was a challenge. "We crossed the river in Wichita
Falls and walked up to the front of this church
building," she said. "It had big wooden doors that were
crooked and couldn't be locked. Instead of pews, there
were only wooden benches." While the church
building was in poor condition, the family was happy

to discover a comfortable and attractive parsonage next door.

Leading up to the 1940 annual conference sessions in Texas, a district superintendent was looking for a pastor to serve a church in Haskell, a county-seat town of about three thousand people, north of Abilene. Reportedly, the superintendent asked Angie Smith at a public meeting what he knew about Kenneth Copeland. Standing within earshot was J. J. "Joe" Perkins, a widely known Methodist philanthropist and influential layman from Wichita Falls. Perkins quickly chimed in, "Kenneth Copeland can be my pastor any day!" With that commendation, the Copelands were soon on their way to First Methodist Church in Haskell.

4

Haskell

oving to Haskell was exciting for the Copeland family, although the first two weeks were a bit rocky. The outgoing pastor refused to move from the parsonage, so the Copeland family initially had to stay elsewhere.

They did eventually occupy the parsonage, which in itself was a benefit and challenge. Catherine remembered with amusement the frequent calls she received from an elderly woman in the congregation. "One day she called to ask if there was a black leather sofa in the parsonage hallway and was perturbed when I said there was not. 'Well, I gave one to the parsonage twenty years ago,' the woman declared. 'I wonder what preacher's wife sold it!'"

Kenneth was delighted to learn that the Haskell church had a pipe organ. When the organist was unable to attend the worship service, he would play. His love of music, nurtured from early childhood, continued to be a source of joy for the minister and those who knew him. He had no formal instruction but could play most hymns and moderately difficult music with little effort. In the evening, he would often play the piano until dinner was served.

For those who considered gospel music unsophisticated and theologically deficient, Kenneth quickly argued that there was nothing wrong with the theology of a song such as "Leaning on the Everlasting Arms." He liked old, familiar songs because they gave personal witness to the love of Christ; he objected to their compartmentalization as gospel music.

> May God help us to cease the misuse of a great word. If "What a Friend We Have in Jesus," is a gospel song, pray tell me what kind of a song is "A Mighty Fortress is Our God"? The Gospel deals first of all with the nature of God who "so loved the world that he gave his only begotten Son, that whosoever believeth in him should not perish, but have everlasting life." The Gospel speaks of a great God, not a limited God.

Sung With Gusto

As a young person, his love of music had endeared him to others and it continued to open doors of enjoyment and influence throughout his life. As word of Kenneth's musical talents spread in Haskell, he was invited to perform at various events in the community. A prominent women's club was among groups asking him to sing. "He'd do nearly anything he was asked to do because he loved it," said Catherine.

Until Kenneth took up the sport of golf in later years, music was his primary recreation. He also enjoyed playing

Forty-two, a domino game popular in Texas. When televisions became commonplace, he acknowledged his enjoyment of western programs such as *Gunsmoke*.

Music is central in the early memories of daughters Patti and Sue, particularly as they recall their dad singing with gusto from the pulpit each Sunday. They also remember music at gatherings of Copeland aunts, uncles, and cousins. "When we had reunions, Saturday night was singing time," said Patti. "We would sit for hours singing one song after another. Daddy and his brothers would sing Stamps-Baxter Quartet songs and 'How Great Thou Art.'"

Patti once went with her dad on an out-of-town speaking engagement. "We got caught in a horrible storm on the way home. Daddy found a filling station with an overhang and pulled under there until the storm passed. We sang and visited and sang and visited. I have never feared storms since. I think it was because of that experience."

Sue sang with Patti and Kenneth while traveling in the car, and later as teenagers when they accompanied their parents to Europe. "Daddy, Patti, and I had a trio, and we sang harmony. I can remember our dirty old train pulling out of the station in Venice. The three of us were hanging out the windows singing some kind of good-bye song to the people. They must have thought we were screwballs, but we had a lot of fun. I don't know who taught us harmony, probably Daddy, as he could sing all the parts."

It was in Haskell that an event known as "dry cleaning the baby" entered into the folklore of Kenneth

Copeland's ministry. A young couple brought their infant daughter to the front of the church for baptism. Kenneth took the baby in his arms and reached into the font, only to realize there was no water. Without hesitation, he cupped his hands in the dry container and proceeded as though water was present. After the service, he shared with Catherine his concern about the baby not having been properly baptized. "As soon as we finished lunch, we went to their home and talked to them about it. Kenneth then baptized the baby with water," Catherine said. The baby's father, a Baptist, said he noticed the absence of water but thought, "Maybe that's the way Methodists do it." The father found the incident amusing.

As was true of all his pastoral appointments, Kenneth did not limit his attention to his congregation but reached into the larger community, becoming active in service clubs and speaking at a wide variety of community functions. In 1943, he was named outstanding citizen of the year by the Haskell Chamber of Commerce.

Kenneth occasionally took one of his young daughters with him while making pastoral visits. After going with her dad to visit a woman with health problems, Sue announced, "Mother, we saw a lady who has nerves."

Many of the girls' early memories were of life in Haskell. Their dad had a practice of remaining at the front of the sanctuary, rather than the entrance, to greet people after worship. Sue would move quickly to his side as soon as the service ended, and hug his leg while he greeted a long line of worshippers.

"I teased him because often people would come and ask him if he remembered them. I could see him squirm and try so hard to remember. His favorite line was, 'Wait a minute, let me see. Let me push the cobwebs back.' He would keep talking and wait until they would say something that would give him a hint as to who they were."

Sue also found amusing her dad's diplomacy when faced with a baby that was not especially pretty. "Now *that's* a baby," she recalled him saying, noncommittally.

A Full-Time Christian

Both Patti and Sue remember his consistency, whether in the pulpit or at the dining table. "He lived every day what he preached on Sunday morning," Patti said. "He was a full-time Christian." Even today, when they must decide if something is worthwhile, Patti and Sue quote their dad's mantra: "Is it true? Is it necessary? Is it kind?"

This consistency in personal and public life was addressed in a newspaper column he wrote later in his ministry: "Following Christ makes a difference in the home. Here, one's religion has its real test. It is not so difficult to put one's best foot forward out in public life, but your own family knows best of all whether or not you are a Christian."

"Early in my life I realized that Daddy really lived what he preached," said Sue. "He was genuine. He believed what he said and he lived it all the time. It was part of everything he did." She said he once spoke to her elementary school class. "I don't know if I volunteered him, but I remember it was the third grade. How proud I was of him."

Kenneth was a diligent record keeper but did not keep a diary. While at Haskell, he listed pastoral visits, including names, purpose, and results. He recorded Bible readings, sermon topics, and prayer concerns. His record of the needs of prospective members included such concerns as "to accept Christ" or "to cease drinking." He was a strong opponent of alcoholic beverages and often spoke out against their sale and use. At least once he spoke at a national meeting of the Women's Christian Temperance Union. "Alcohol is pervasive and destructive in modern society," he once said. "It is a sedative, a retreat, and a stumbling block that keeps us from the victorious life."

His record of performing marriages showed that he received fees ranging from two to five dollars. Catherine told with amusement the story of a wedding ceremony in the parsonage after which the groom asked how much he owed the pastor for his service. When told there was no charge, the young man produced a one-dollar bill and said, "Well, I know she's worth a dollar."

Kenneth's records show that of his $250-a-month salary, he gave a $25 tithe. He sometimes identified how the tithe money was distributed, with such notations as "colored church," and "Methodist Youth Fellowship." In one instance, he paid the bail for someone in the community.

The Copelands lived in Haskell during some of the most difficult years of World War II. Like many men his age, Kenneth felt the need to go into military service, even though clergymen were exempt. "He felt he had something to offer in the military and he had a great concern for the men," Catherine said. "We discussed it and it was all right with me if he decided to go." Kenneth's bishop convinced him otherwise, saying that the best place for him to serve his country, the servicemen, and their families was to remain a pastor in the local church.

Kenneth went to great lengths to identify with the concerns, issues, and heartaches of his church members. A cotton grower in the Haskell congregation was unable to find workers at a crucial time, so Kenneth, Catherine, and the girls put on work clothes and went to the fields. "We picked cotton for two days," recalled Catherine. "I doubt that we made a big difference, but he was in trouble. We tried to do our part to help."

Kenneth's pastoral spirit, keen sensitivity, and compassion were evident not only in his preaching, counseling, and interpersonal contacts, but also in his writings. He often wrote letters to friends and family members who were facing difficulties or dealing with tragedies. One letter was written to his brother Bill, who was superintendent of schools at Mt. Vernon, Texas.

Bill had given his approval in the afternoon of September 20, 1959, for his grade school principal to drive a school bus of students to see a junior high football game in Cooper, forty miles away. The bus was involved in a highway accident; the driver, a teacher, and six children were killed.

The undated, two-page letter Kenneth sent to Bill was simply headed, "Tuesday morning. In my study." In it, he addressed the concerns and questions that people continue to ask today when tragedy strikes.

> We cannot afford to punish ourselves with probing questions that ask again and again, "Is there something I might have done, some decision that I might have made, that would have prevented this tragedy?" Limited human beings that we are, we can usually look back and see some little thing here and there that might have made the difference. But we must remember that we acted, in that given situation, according to the best knowledge we had at the time. Had we known then what we know now, of course, we could have done differently. But we cannot afford to punish ourselves with feelings of guilt of any kind when we did what we thought was right at the moment. We cannot go back and undo the past. When we have acted in accordance with what knowledge and judgment we had at the time, then we must leave those results in the hands of a good God who understands where we cannot.

Kenneth addressed the question of why God allows accidents to happen.

> In a limited world, with limited human beings who cannot possibly foresee everything and every condition, accidents will happen. Accidents . . . are a part of our limited knowledge and limited power. An accident is something God does not order and man cannot foresee and does not choose. They come as the result of the accumulation of a number of factors which, in our limited knowledge, collide at certain places with tragic results.

GOD DID NOT INTEND THIS TO HAPPEN. God does not order tragedy! There are certain physical factors we can see involved in the collision of two automobiles, the limited judgment of drivers, the speed of the vehicles, etc. . . . God permits these tragedies. For an answer to the "why" here, we are still searching, but perhaps will not fully understand until we are housed with him in the eternal city of God where vision is unlimited.

Kenneth assured his brother that while God did not order the tragedy, God is not powerless in such a time.

In all things, God works with those who love him to bring about that which is good. God was right in the middle of the cross, and out of it came the salvation of the world. It is hard to see this when the tragedy has come to our own doorstep, but faith furnishes the power to accept it, even when we cannot see it, and from that start we can go on to victory, through his help.

When in the midst of heartache and tragedy we say, "Thy will, O God, be done," we do not mean simply that we accept the tragedy as something we cannot now change. We mean, "O God, thy will be done in me and in all those who are affected by this experience. Thy will be done in our minds and hearts as we walk through this valley of the shadow of death." For God has a will for us in our relation to the tragedy and what we make of it in our daily lives.

Kenneth assured Bill that God weeps in times of human heartache.

Jesus joined in the sorrow of the sisters of Lazarus when, at his grave, he also wept. This was no show of emotion for the benefit of the crowd. The tears of Jesus were real, for his heart sorrowed more deeply than the hearts of Mary and Martha could possibly have done. Likewise, in our human griefs he sorrows with us, and in that sharing experience he becomes one with us in both our grief and in the strength he gives to transform grief into spiritual gain.

Kenneth received his next pastoral appointment in 1944 at the invitation of his good friend Angie Smith. Smith had been elected a bishop earlier that year at the South Central Jurisdictional Conference and was assigned to the Oklahoma Area. Very soon after moving to Oklahoma, Smith asked Kenneth to become senior pastor of the 1,851-member First Methodist Church in Stillwater, home of Oklahoma A&M (now Oklahoma State University). Catherine's initial response to the move was, "Oh, if it were only in Texas." But she and family, consistent with their understanding of the itinerant ministry of Methodist preachers, were soon packing for their move to Stillwater, and looking forward to a new chapter in their lives together. Patti was ten; Sue, seven.

5

Stillwater

Kenneth Copeland observed in later years that serving the Stillwater congregation was one of his most difficult challenges because of the wide educational range of its members. At the same time, he relished work with university faculty and students at the college. For Patti and Sue, Stillwater was an immediate hit. Upon their arrival in the city, shortly after dark, they spotted not one but two movie theaters.

For the first time, Kenneth served a congregation large enough to require two Sunday morning worship services. As he had done in previous churches, he preached each Sunday evening as well. Most of the college students attended the first service, which was broadcast over a local radio station. Overflow rooms were equipped with speakers to accommodate those who came too late to find seating in the sanctuary.

Kenneth's reputation as a speaker and preacher spread rapidly throughout Oklahoma. He was asked to speak at community events and in other churches. He led study courses for pastors at Oklahoma City University. His record of engagements showed that he spoke at the chambers of commerce; service clubs; American Legion posts; PTAs; fraternities and sororities; Wesley Foundations; Boy Scout gatherings; and even elementary classrooms, where his topic was often "joy." He spoke to a Catholic group in Stillwater, using the topic, "Mary Pondered These Things."

Even though he had been in the East Oklahoma Conference for fewer than four years, his popularity among his clergy colleagues was evident. He was elected the first reserve delegate to the 1948 South Central Jurisdictional Conference in El Paso. At that time, the East Oklahoma Conference had three clergy delegates to the general conference and six to the jurisdictional conference.

Kenneth earned his bachelor of arts degree from Southern Methodist University while serving in Dallas and later took graduate courses at Garrett Biblical Institute in Evanston, Illinois. He never earned a seminary degree, however. This lack of a formal seminary education didn't threaten his self-image or lessen his confidence as a Bible scholar and preacher. He was invited to lecture at seminaries and in other educational institutions. He was a disciplined scholar from the days as his father's associate at Corsicana through his service as bishop. In all his pastoral appointments, he had breakfast with the family and then secluded himself in his parsonage office for prayer, reflection, and study before going to the church. Family members knew that when he was in his study, they were not to intrude, except for emergencies.

Asked if her father ever expressed concern about not having a seminary degree, Sue, a professional family counselor, said, "I don't think he was a person of low self-esteem about anything, but he didn't feel he was above anybody, either." She said he treated the church custodian with as much respect and dignity as any church official or political dignitary. "I never felt he was being condescending. It was genuine."

Sue said her decision to be a counselor was influenced greatly by the respectful way her father related to others. "The way he treated people was a big influence on me. Even before I went into the counseling profession, I remember how important it was for me to be genuine with people, to be real. That's what he was. He didn't put on airs. He had a way of cutting through to what was real."

Neither Sue nor Patti remembers a time when they were embarrassed or hesitant about having a preacher as their father. "Daddy was always loved, so our family was loved," said Sue. "It was a privilege for me to go with him when he would preach. He was a powerful preacher. Often I was personally moved by his preaching, even as a child. He lived it, so it was believable for me. Authentic, that's what he was and what I've wanted to be."

"I was very proud of my daddy," said Patti. "He was so well thought of by the people in the community, not just for his preaching but for his attitude and his fun. He was loved by everyone. That felt good to me."

In 1945, Kenneth led a seminar on recreation for young people at St. Luke's Methodist Church in Oklahoma City. One of the teenage participants told him he wanted to attend Oklahoma A&M but couldn't due to a shortage of rooms. Kenneth invited the young man to move in with the Copelands.

In a 1993 letter of appreciation, that man, Franklin Springer, wondered how Catherine, Patti, and Sue received the news that a young man would be moving into a spare bedroom, sharing the family's one bathroom, and eating breakfast in a booth built for four.

Springer lived with the Copelands during the spring and fall semesters of 1946. He fondly recalled Kenneth playing the piano and enthusiastically singing another verse of "Hold the Fort For I Am Coming" (Philip Bliss, 1870). Springer also recalled the importance of giving Kenneth his space for study and reflection. "When he closed the French doors into his parsonage office, and we heard the clacking of the typewriter, we knew it would be another special three-point sermon complete with alliterations." (Kenneth had taught himself to type using what Catherine described as a two-finger method.)

Kenneth Copeland's combination of dignity and humor changed the image of a preacher for many Stillwater citizens, Springer said. "If there is such a thing as pragmatic compassion, Kenneth practiced it. He could just sit down alongside and bring comfort to us with his well-practiced faith. He knew how to help bridge the rough waters."

Theodore Agnew and his wife, Jeanne, moved to Stillwater in 1947, and joined First Church in March

1948. "We lost a newborn child in January of that year, and Dr. Copeland helped us through that bereavement," Agnew said. "He was revered by my generation as a great spiritual preacher. He was good at sustaining, nurturing, and building up the congregation."

Agnew remembered Kenneth arriving early to speak at a men's dinner at the church and writing his sermon notes on the butcher paper tablecloth spread on the long tables.

After being elected a bishop, Kenneth returned to Stillwater for a preaching mission and went to the Agnew home for a meal. Agnew recalled:

> He captivated our kids with stories. One was a charade. He asked us to bring in an axe. Fortunately we had one. Then he asked for two or three potatoes, which Jeanne produced. The bishop put them on the axe and asked, "What great scholarly work does this represent?" Nobody knew. "Why, it's simple," he said. "Common taters on the axe, fifth book of the New Testament." After some good-humored groans, Bishop Copeland asked, "What do you call potatoes in Ireland?" Nobody knew. "Why, of course," he said, "you don't call them, you dig them."

Just as he used humor to communicate, Kenneth embraced the mass media of his day—newspapers, radio, and television—to expand his proclamation of the gospel. In January 1949, his last year at Stillwater, he gave five meditations on radio station KSPI with the theme, "Challenge to Real Living."

"We prepare for life physically, mentally, and socially, but making spiritual preparation seems to be an unnecessary burden to so many," he told his radio audience. "The reason some of us get so little out of life," he declared, "is because we put so little into it." Stressing the importance of beginning each day with spiritual preparation, he observed, "People who never learn how to pray when the sun is shining have the most difficulty learning it in a storm."

He called on his listeners to have courage as they sought to live meaningful lives. "It takes real courage for youth of our generation to stand for principles of purity and truth when they see so much in our lives that indicates a total disregard for these same principles."

His meditations included a challenge to follow Christ and experience faith. "This faith in Christ is a faith that actually works!" he declared. "God is no theory. He is energy, power, strength, courage. And all this came to us in Jesus Christ. 'I can do all things through Christ who strengthens me,' says the apostle, and so can you. There is no reason for anyone of you to live any longer in fear."

He stressed the importance of both belief and action, a frequent theme of his ministry. "It is impossible to live greatly without believing greatly," he said. "And do not allow yourself to believe the age-old glib statement: 'It doesn't matter what you believe, so long as you are sincere and trying to do the right thing.' I don't think you will do the right thing unless you believe the right thing." At the same time, he said faith is more than belief. "Seeing it plainly, faith is a living function involving our lives in God's purpose in such a way that he becomes involved in our lives. In other words, faith is not only belief but action, and action is possible only when trust precedes it. One who really believes in God will trust God and act upon his promises."

Kenneth's sermons usually closed with a call for a personal commitment to Christ. In church settings, these often took the form of altar calls, a practice he continued throughout his ministry, even as a bishop, and even in situations and regions where they were uncommon.

During his five years at Stillwater, the church prospered, with membership growing from 1,851 to 2,338. Early in 1949, in the middle of the conference year, Kenneth was asked to go to Travis Park Methodist Church in San Antonio. Bishop W. Angie Smith's brother, Bishop A. Frank Smith, contacted Kenneth about the opening, and the appointment was made not only with Bishop Angie's blessing, but also with his encouragement.

Catherine said Bishop Angie advised Kenneth to get a haircut, shine his shoes, and fly to San Antonio in style. Kenneth, an immaculate dresser, didn't need the advice, but he and Catherine flew to San Antonio and made a quick and positive impression on Travis Park's pastor-parish relations committee.

When the Stillwater congregation gathered to say good-bye, Judge W. H. Wilcox, chairman of the official board, paid tribute to the Copelands and praised Kenneth's talents as a preacher:

He has held before us God's holy book and the simple message of salvation. Therein has rested the secret of the success of his preaching—always for a verdict and never failing to win a verdict, more often then not in the ready and open acceptance by someone, young or old, to the call to come to the altar and there to publicly repent of sins and confess guilt and believe on the Lord Jesus Christ for salvation. What a winsome Gospel he has preached! No wonder the membership rolls of the church have been increased by hundreds during his ministry.

Kenneth preached his first sermon at Travis Park on March 9, 1949. His topic was "Facing the Future With Faith." Earlier that week, the *Travis Park News* (March 4), included a photo of the family and a letter from M. A. Beeson, a member of the Stillwater congregation, lay leader for the East Oklahoma Conference, and a professor at A&M.

It is a blow to lose Brother Copeland, for he is the greatest pastor of my life experience. In fact, I consider him the most versatile and strongest young minister in Methodism. He has a brilliant mind, and everything that touches it sticks and it sticks right side up. He has a warm heart like John Wesley after his Aldersgate Street experience. He is humble and approachable. He has a sympathetic and understanding heart and mind, never too busy or worn to minister to anyone in need. He has courage to stand for the right, but always with a kind and gentle spirit that wins.

During his four-and-a-half years here, he has won the respect and confidence of the town and college. People in all walks of life love him for his consecrated life, his sincerity, and his messages.

STILLWATER

Above all, he loves Christ with a consuming passion and loves to lead men and women to Christ. Last week someone asked him to go see the owner of one of our leading hotels who was ill, and while visiting him, the man was led to Christ and wanted to be baptized and join the church. Brother Copeland took him into the church (membership) at the hotel and his wife asked to be transferred from another church to the Methodist Church to be with her husband. In addition to these, five were taken into the church at the Sunday morning services: the head of a department at the college and his wife from another denomination, where they had their membership before coming to Stillwater; an army officer who transferred his membership from a church of another denomination in his home town; a student who transferred from his home town church; and a student by profession of faith. This was not an exceptional week.

He is an excellent speaker at civic clubs and youth gatherings. In fact, he is good anywhere, whether in public or private. He can appeal to the great and humble alike in his addresses and personal contacts. He can lead the singing and play the piano and pipe organ.

Our church is mourning his departure. A college professor, who was trying to comfort us, said that we should be thankful that we have been able to keep him as long as we have. We are sad because of his leaving, but rejoice that he is going to Travis Park Church with its great opportunities and where there is a staff sufficient to relieve him of much of the detail work of the program of the church, thus giving him more time for private devotion, study, personal contacts, preaching, and public addresses. He is a choice soul and deserves the best, and I am sure you will love him as all do who know him.

Too many good things cannot be said about Mrs. Copeland. She is a pastor's ideal wife, a woman of refinement, culture, poise, and good judgment, knowing what to say under all circumstances. She is charming, capable, and devout, and everyone loves her. She is a good speaker, also.

Patti and Sue, their two daughters, are lovely girls whom you will love and enjoy.

Our great loss is your gain.

Bereft at losing the Copelands, one member of the Stillwater congregation reportedly said, "Well, what Texas giveth, Texas taketh away!"

6

San Antonio

At the age of thirty-six, Kenneth Copeland assumed the leadership of the 5,246-member Travis Park Methodist Church in downtown San Antonio, one of the ten largest congregations in the denomination. The appointment provided him twelve years of ministry, the longest tenure in his career, and ushered him into Methodism's highest office.

Kenneth's Oklahoma Area bishop and friend Angie Smith was known widely for his leadership style—described by some as strongly self-confident and by others as arbitrary. Bishop Roy H. Short, in his *History of the Council of Bishops*, described Smith as a bishop who always knew where he wanted to go and how to get there.

Many found the close friendship between Kenneth and Angie Smith puzzling, because their leadership styles were so dramatically different. Their relationship undoubtedly was based in part on their shared passion for preaching and evangelism. Bishop Short said Smith "wrote an enviable record of reaching large numbers of people for Christ, not only in the churches that he served, but also through the definite evangelistic plans that he developed constantly for his area." The same could be said about Kenneth. Smith gave strong church-wide leadership in evangelism, serving for eight years as president of the Methodist Board of Evangelism. Just before his election as bishop, Kenneth served eight years on the Methodist Board of Evangelism. Later he was a member of the United Methodist Board of Discipleship, which included evangelism programming.

Travis Park, the mother church of San Antonio Methodism, was organized in 1846, a few months after Texas statehood. During Kenneth's tenure as the church's forty-seventh senior pastor, fifteen individuals from the congregation entered full-time Christian service and 3,549 new members were received, more than a third of whom professed Christian faith publicly for the first time.

Construction of a youth building began in 1948 and was completed the year the Copelands arrived. The formal opening was on January 8, 1950. The building included classrooms, worship centers, and recreational facilities, mainly for youth, but also a bride's room and a chapel that could seat one hundred seventy people.

No colleague at Travis Park knew Kenneth better than Betty Ann Janert, his secretary during his twelve years at the church. She had joined the staff at age sixteen, and two years later, she became secretary to the new pastor. "He was so young we didn't know quite what to expect, but we soon came to love him," she said. Kenneth once noticed that Janert was struggling to find scriptural references. He gave her a small concordance. Inside the cover he wrote, "Seek and ye shall find!"

Kenneth rarely preached from a manuscript, preferring to use an outline written on a single sheet of paper, folded once. Hundreds of these sermon notes remain in files today, some written on hotel stationery. Sermons for special occasions were printed and available for church members. After becoming a bishop, he provided manuscripts of addresses given at large public gatherings, mostly to assist newspaper reporters covering the events.

The new pastor, however, had to be reminded that the large church had a multiple staff and that he didn't have to do everything for himself, Janert said. "He wanted to answer and acknowledge every piece of correspondence. We wrote a letter in response to everybody, even someone who sent him a picture postcard from their recent vacation. He also did a great deal of counseling, not only of members but also people from the community."

After a church member had been especially rude to Kenneth, Janert said a staff member asked him, "Why don't you tell him off?" Kenneth replied, "But what if his wife dies tonight?"

Irene Cox Wischer, an active lay member at Travis Park, said of Kenneth, "If there ever was a perfect man, he was one. He loved fun, ministry, family. He related so well to people." She praised Catherine as a skilled communicator who possessed great compassion.

Wischer's first husband, Milton Cox, played golf with Kenneth every Saturday, when possible. "Milton would come home saying he felt like he had played golf with the Lord," she said.

She praised Kenneth's preaching skills and pastoral sensitivities. "He sat with my mother in the hospital when she was ill and was expected to die. He wouldn't leave. Even after he went to Nebraska, he called me when he learned of the deaths of my husband and mother."

Like parishioners in all the churches Kenneth served, Wischer remembered his signature white shirts. "Even if we were to go to their house unexpectedly, he would come into the room wearing a white shirt," she said.

Kenneth's reputation as a real dresser is remembered by Leonard Davis, a San Antonio attorney who was a young adult member at Travis Park in the 1950s. "At the invitation of somebody at Lackland Air Force Base, Dr. Copeland led a session for a large group of officers on how to dress and behave as gentlemen."

Davis recalled a story told by Kenneth after his election as bishop: "A porter on the railroad kept calling him 'Mr. President.' Finally Bishop Copeland told him, 'I'm not a president. I'm a bishop of the Methodist Church.' The porter looked him over and observed, 'I knew whatever you were in, you were in charge of.'"

As was the custom of the day, he was known by many of his parishioners as "Brother Copeland. In 1951 he was given an honorary doctor of divinity degree by Methodist-related Southwestern University in Georgetown, Texas, and became "Dr. Copeland."

Kenneth gave meditations on San Antonio radio stations and appeared on interfaith television programs featuring him, a Catholic priest, and a Jewish rabbi. Sunday morning services at Travis Park were also televised.

Parishioner Wischer was influential in getting the *San Antonio Express* newspaper to carry Kenneth's daily "Learning to Live" column. It appeared in each weekday issue beginning on January 1, 1959, until he left Travis Park in late 1960. The short messages addressed topics such as breaking bad habits, intercessory prayer, honoring parents, forgiveness, marriage, family life, and overcoming fear.

A theme woven through many of the columns was the importance of not being self-centered. "To have friends means being a friend to others," he wrote. "One good way to be a friend is to be more interested in what you can give others than in what you can get from others. And then, it would help if you would spend more time thanking God for what others are doing for you than in complaining of what others are doing to you. Others have done so much for you, more than you will ever be able to repay."

In one series of columns on "Thanks," Kenneth urged his readers to turn their thoughts outward. "Give attention to the needs of others more than to your own needs. Seek not so much to be understood as to understand, not so much to be ministered unto as to minister, not so much to get as to give. Then try turning your thoughts upward instead of downward. Of course there is much sorrow and heartache in this world, but there is perfect peace and victory with God."

In another series, he addressed the importance of growing up. "The immature person always has 'I' at the center, and if he ever thinks of anyone else it is only casually. You can rest assured, however, that when a person endeavors honestly and sincerely to put God at the center, others next, and self last, he is maturing."

Self-examination should always precede caustic criticisms of others, he declared in another column. "We are not to cast stones at others unless we know we are without sin. . . . We need the mirror of God's Word to help us to see ourselves not as others see us, but as we really are. We can do little toward removing the logs from our eyes until we know they are there, recognize their presence, and pray for God's help in taking them away."

The columns were enthusiastically received by *Express* readers. In the newspaper's May 19, 1959 issue, editors wrote: "Since San Antonio's Dr. Kenneth Copeland began writing inspirational messages five days a week for the *Express* beginning January 1, we have received many messages from readers thanking him and us for this contribution to their spiritual life."

The editorial told of a reader who carried a particular column in his billfold; another who sent the columns to a family member having difficulties; a patient who tacked columns on her hospital wall; and a reader who was putting the columns in a scrapbook. Because of the columns, one couple unrelated to Travis Park reported they had gone to Kenneth for counseling in an effort to save their troubled marriage.

During the time Kenneth was pastor at Travis Park Church, the nation experienced a surge of anti-Communism. With the war going badly in Korea and Communist advances in Eastern Europe, the American people were genuinely frightened about the possibilities of internal subversion. A key figure of the period was Joseph McCarthy. This senator from Wisconsin chaired a committee that investigated government departments and questioned people about their political pasts. People from all walks of life became the subject of aggressive witch-hunts, often based on inconclusive or questionable evidence.

In 1950, *Reader's Digest* carried an article, "Methodism's Pink Fringe," which charged that organizations within Methodism, the largest Protestant church in the United States, were filled with Communists and fellow travelers [a term for those sympathetic to Communist causes].

In 1952, the House Committee on Un-American Activities issued an eight-page pamphlet, *Review of the Methodist Federation for Social Action*, charging that the organization generally followed the Communist party line. Among those defending themselves before the House Committee was G. Bromley Oxnam, a Methodist bishop serving in Washington, D.C.

The Methodist Council of Bishops released a statement in 1953 concerning the charges. "We resent unproven assertions that the Protestant ministry is honeycombed with disloyalty. We are unalterably opposed to Communism, but we know that the alternative to Communism is not an American brand of fascism."

While he was not hesitant to speak out against Communism, Kenneth warned that it was but one among many evils that threatened American freedom and values. In a sermon at Travis Park soon after the election of President Dwight D. Eisenhower, he said, "Phantoms of fear and foes of freedom, both within and without our national life, threaten the spiritual security and moral stability that have made this nation great."

He condemned Communism for its "relentless attempt to destroy America" and its godless ideology that "owes no allegiance to truth, honor, honesty, or virtue, since these are attributes of God and exist only as a part of His law in the universe." But, he emphasized, other evils threatening America included "secularism, materialism, selfishness, complacency, greed, prejudice, bigotry, lust, and drunkenness."

> We cannot wash our hands in innocence simply because we are trying to hold Communism back. What has happened to our sense of values? We spend more than nine billion dollars for liquor each year in this country, and about one-third that amount for education and religion. While the liquor industry spends millions annually for advertising, we have to beg for the nickels and dollars for foreign missions.

SAN ANTONIO

We speak of security for America and spend billions for defense, while little more than half of our population confesses any allegiance to any religious institution. . . . Of course America must be protected, and we must be prepared against any emergency. But, don't you think we are very foolish if we believe for one fleeting moment that the only security we need is that fastened to the belly of a plane or locked in the explosive of an atomic bomb? Let us wake up and realize ours must be, first of all, a security of spiritual values. God forbid that we should lose ourselves in a spiritual drowsiness.

Political and personal security were but two of many issues which church members confronted with the guidance and direction of their pastor. Kenneth took seriously his role as shepherd of his flock. No event challenged him more than a devastating fire which struck Travis Park Church in the early hours of October 25, 1955. A church member, a pharmacist in a nearby shop, sounded the alarm about six thirty in the morning. The fire started in the basement and burned through the sanctuary floor, destroying the organ, some pews, and part of the altar rail, making the entire building useless.

Kenneth later described rushing to the scene:

> After parking as close as I could and coming in view of the church, my eyes caught first of all the devastating sight of smoke billowing from the windows, the roof, and the sides of the church. Those of you who have faced

scenes like that in your own home or the institution so beloved to your heart can imagine the pain and passion that stirred my soul and saddened my heart when I had to stand and look at a scene like that.

The fire was especially tragic in that major renovations had been underway in the facilities for several years. More than $142,000 had been spent just three years earlier to air condition the sanctuary, main building, and children's building.

The first Sunday after the fire, the morning worship service was held in the Municipal Auditorium; the evening service was held at First Presbyterian Church. A Jewish rabbi was one of the first of many religious and community leaders to offer the congregation facilities and assistance.

In *Growing a Soul*, the biography of Bishop A. Frank Smith, written by Norman W. Spellmann in 1979, Kenneth told how he turned to his bishop for guidance after the fire:

> I knew that we had to rebuild or move and build brand new. Either way, it meant a long financial campaign. I had never been a builder of churches, and I really faced my moment of greatest frustration. So I called Bishop Smith and asked if Catherine and I could come down to see him. We set a day and drove down to Houston. And I said, "Bishop, this is the first time in my life that I have really wanted to run." And I'll never forget. He stood up and put that large hand on my shoulder and said: "Now, Kenneth, let me just say something to you. You have laymen in your church and on your board who know more about

raising money and architectural drawings and building than you will ever need to know. That's not your business. You advise with them about the religious significance of the building, but your main job is to hold that congregation together. It's your business to love them, preach to them, pastor them, and advise with your committees. If you do that, they will build the church." Well, I went back convinced that I was going to prove that his judgment was right if it killed me. And it didn't kill me, and his judgment was right. That was a crisis point at which he very gently, lovingly, and tenderly held me in check. I had no need to run.

Copeland told Bishop Smith's biographer that the bishop "always found time to let a preacher who was hurting come in and talk with him."

Church officers presented several options to the congregation, including relocation to the suburbs, but the decision was made to remain downtown. Rebuilding and repairs took almost three years and cost $1.5 million. A clergy colleague suggested that with all the added responsibilities, Kenneth might need to dig old sermons out of a barrel, but Catherine said that wasn't the case. "He preached a new sermon every Sunday."

Church offices moved to the youth building, which had received the least damage, but Sunday morning worship services were held in the Texas Theatre, almost two blocks away. Evening services were held at nearby St. Mark's Episcopal Church. Patti married during this time; the ceremony was held at St. Mark's.

Displaced adult church school classes met all over the neighborhood: in the Gunter and St. Anthony hotels, the YMCA, and in office buildings. Despite the inconvenience, there were few complaints, according to secretary Janert. There was even humor in the experience. She said the congregation arrived for worship at the Texas Theater one Sunday morning and found a prize-winning steer from the San Antonio Fat Stock Show tethered in the lobby. She also recalled the squeaking of the machinery that elevated the choir from the orchestra pit to stage level.

When the remodeled sanctuary and new educational building were completed in September 1958, the total value of the Travis Park property was about $3 million. At that point, Travis Park had 4,500 members. The Travis Park building was designated a historical site by the Texas State Historical Commission in 1974, and by the United Methodist General Commission on Archives and History in 1980.

In his first Sunday sermon after the fire, "Rebuilding the Walls," Kenneth urged the congregation to use the Book of Nehemiah for guidance. "How did these defeated, dislodged, and disappointed people under Nehemiah's leadership rebuild the wall of Jerusalem?" he asked. Following their example, he said, would require from Travis Park members deathless love, a mind to work, a spirit to cooperate, and a sense of divine mission.

Kenneth shared a story that would be told and retold by Travis Park members and recorded for posterity. A Catholic bellboy at St. Anthony Hotel requested extra work for the day and brought seven dollars in tips to the church office. "It did not amount to much as far as dollars and cents were concerned," Kenneth said, "but it amounted to a tremendous lot as far as the spirit of goodwill and love and a mind to work."

He challenged members to "lay aside every 'sin that doth so easily beset us' . . . every prejudice, every selfish jealousy, every humanistic element of selfishness and rise as one . . . behind our Lord Jesus Christ as a vital organism to meet this hour unafraid and unashamed . . . a willingness to cooperate."

Typical of his ability to use humor, even in the bleakest circumstances, he told of people in a small community, including the pastor, joining a bucket brigade to put out a fire at the Methodist Church.

> To his astonishment and amazement the pastor noticed beside him the town's chief cynic, who never came to church, helping to pass water in the bucket brigade. The pastor was a bit amused and had to pause long enough in the midst of the tragedy to say, "Well, brother, this is the first time I have ever seen you at the Methodist Church." The man replied, "This is the first time the Methodist Church has ever been on fire."

"The fire is a tragedy," Kenneth said, "but let it be a symbol of the fact that whether or not this is the first time, that this is one time that Travis Park Methodist Church is on fire for Christ and the Kingdom."

Regarding a sense of mission, he pointed to Nehemiah telling his opponents that he didn't have time to talk to them: "I am doing a great work, and I cannot come down. Why should the work stop while I leave it and come down to you. I am doing a great work—I cannot come down."

Praising that spirit of mission, Kenneth declared, "We are doing a great work here. Nothing must interfere, nothing must stop it, and by the grace of God nothing will stop it. This Church has never been as united as it is now."

Upon completion of the rebuilding project, Kenneth challenged his flock to "be a part of the real body of Christ, speaking with his voice, serving with his hands, and living and breathing with his Spirit. To this high purpose, may the Christ this day consecrate the church."

The fire may have been the greatest test of Kenneth's leadership skills at Travis Park, but the church's ministry with young people was among his greatest achievements. During the Korean War, young adults, including college students and soldiers, flocked to Travis Park.

Annedelle Fincher Brantley directed the church's youth program during Kenneth's first six years in San Antonio. She had been a member of his congregation in Stillwater while a student at Oklahoma A&M. "I was planning to be a home economics teacher, but Dr. Copeland called and persuaded me to come work with youth. I'm glad I did. It was a rewarding experience," she said. A new, three-story youth building was under construction when she arrived in 1949. She married David A. "Tony" Brantley, one of the young adults at Travis Park, in 1955. He retired in 1979, after twenty-five years as a United Methodist clergy member of the Southwest Texas Annual Conference.

The youth building became home away from home for many young people in the 1950s, especially after the closing of a local service center for military personnel. "We drew men and women from several military bases in the area," said Brantley. After military service, many of the men stayed in San Antonio, some to attend college.

Many of those who were in the older youth department are now in their seventies and return for regular reunions to reflect on their formative years at Travis Park. A member of the Copelands's extended family attended the 2003 reunion. When he asked one of the participants from a distant state what motivated him to be there, the quick response was "Dr. Copeland."

Leonard Davis, who was stationed at Lackland Air Force Base from 1951 to 1955, attended a recent reunion at Mt. Wesley, a Methodist campsite near Kerrville, Texas. He said there were surprised expressions on the faces of the staff as gray-haired people started showing up for an event reserved for the "Travis Park Youth Group."

Brantley was the central figure that guided the youth and young adult program, Davis said. "She was the kind of person who made you feel good about yourself. She and Dr. Copeland were good listeners. She was sincere and warm-hearted and interested in us." She kept in touch with members of the group as they literally moved around the world. Some were stationed elsewhere but later returned to San Antonio and rejoined the group.

"Annedelle always had us doing something," Davis said. "I remember that she had about thirty of us working for a day or two digging and pouring the foundation for a small Methodist church on the outskirts of the city. Women of the church made pies for us."

Stanley "Swede" Erickson, a retired United Methodist minister who now lives in Florence, Texas, was one of those introduced to Christian faith and church membership at Travis Park.

After a three-year stint in England, he was stationed at Kelly Air Force Base in San Antonio in late 1953. He went into the city on a Wednesday night to find an ice-skating rink. As people were leaving Travis Park Church, "I asked one of the ladies how to get to the rink. She gave me the directions, and in that short conversation encouraged me to visit the church's college-age group."

Erickson laughed at the idea of his going to a church for any reason, but a few weeks later he woke up on a Sunday morning, lonely and with a hangover. He remembered the invitation to Travis Park and decided to check it out. "I thought maybe I could meet some girls," he recalled, laughing. "I was twenty-one."

Despite some initial embarrassment, he soon became part of the group. He was baptized and became a member of the church. But the movement of the Spirit in his life didn't stop there. As he and other young people were listening to some missionaries on furlough from Bolivia, Erickson said he felt something. "I didn't hear voices. I may have been daydreaming, but all of a sudden I felt I ought to go into the ministry. I was the most unlikely candidate to go into the ministry you can imagine. You might as well have told me I would be a ballet dancer."

He sought out Brantley. She suggested that he talk with Wayne Banks, the church's minister of education. "I went to his house at dinnertime," he said. "I had never been to a minister's house. I expected to hear chimes."

Banks told Erickson he should visit with Kenneth Copeland. *Oh, sure!* he thought. "Dr. Copeland was, to me, like one of the apostles. He was *Doctor* Copeland, the man of this big church. Me, talk to him? I was still drinking, not a drunk, but just a normal guy."

Nevertheless, he made an appointment with the senior pastor. "I was so nervous going into his office. It was like a throne room to me. I told him I thought I was cracking up. I told him I didn't hear any voice, but I felt a call to ministry."

He said Kenneth prayed with him and advised him not to make a quick decision. "He told me to pray. If the call was real, he said it would happen again." But Erickson wasn't sure about prayer. "As I left his office, I thought, *Yeah, pray about it!* I didn't know how to pray. The only prayers I knew were, 'Now I lay me down to sleep,' or 'Be present at our table, Lord.'"

He went back to Brantley and Banks, and told them he didn't know how to pray. At their suggestion, he joined a prayer group, which he found more frustrating than helpful. "I finally gave myself a month to hear something," he said. "I thought I was going crazy.

I had been an amateur boxer, and I thought maybe I had been punched too hard in the head."

A short time later, he and the Travis Park young people went to a meeting at Abilene Christian College. "It was just before lunch; I was listening to the speaker. I was also thinking about wanting to eat and hoping I might get to sit next to a particular girl. All of a sudden—no voice, no banging on my head, no ringing of chimes—I just felt like I ought to go into ministry."

Again, he sought out Brantley. "I told her I had received my calling and I was going into ministry. It changed my whole life then and there."

After completing military duty, he earned his undergraduate degree at Trinity University in San Antonio. He worked a year before attending Perkins School of Theology in Dallas; he graduated in 1964. Since then he has served as a chaplain and pastor. He was pastor of the Florence United Methodist Church before retiring in 1998.

When he learned that a book was being written about Kenneth Copeland, Erickson suggested it be titled *The Thirteenth Apostle*.

"When I think of him, I still get a lump in my throat, because he's still in my mind: the great Dr. Copeland who blew my mind. And Mrs. Copeland, she's an absolute saint. I don't know anybody in our group who wouldn't give their life for her, literally."

Brantley and Janert are quick to speak of Kenneth's popularity with the young adults. "He was such a friend and positive example that to this day they hold

him as the epitome of good preaching and a good man
. . . and his wife as well," Brantley said.

Don Frizzle was another member of the Travis Park
older youth department in the 1950s. He retired in 1989
as superintendent of schools in Amherst, Massachusetts.
"I came from a poor family in New England with no
college aspirations. My goal was to be a storekeeper. I
got the idea for further education when I went to Texas
and became part of the Travis Park group. Thank
heaven for Dr. Copeland and for Annedelle. It was the
group she put together that helped me figure out what
it was all about."

Most of the Travis Park group went into professions
that serve society—clergy, doctors, lawyers, and professors, Frizzle said. "I don't think we would have done
that if it hadn't been for Dr. Copeland. He pushed our
horizons forward and helped us set a direction for who
we were to become. We were just regular guys who
were in the right place at the right time."

"J-O-Y" was the young adult group's motto, one that
still has deep meaning for Frizzle. "J stands for Jesus first;
O for others second; and Y for yourself third. The spirit of
that brought us all together in a kind of connectedness."

Kenneth Copeland was a central figure in that
connectedness. "His message to us was always one of
love and caring," said Frizzle. "He was a bright man but
very close to the emotions of people. We were all away
from our regular lives, and he made us feel at home. He
had a wonderful family."

Frizzle also praised Brantley's leadership skills.
"She wasn't much older than we were, but she had

an immense spirituality about her and a capacity for caring."

A highlight of Frizzle's week in those years was Sunday morning worship at Travis Park.

It was an enormously popular place at the time. Hundreds of people were there. Most of the students would jam into the balcony. The power of Dr. Copeland's delivery as a preacher was immense. He would call people down to the altar to renew their faith. He was so personal about it. I came from a small New England Methodist church that didn't have much emotion to it. To go to a place like this, with hundreds present and many going down to the altar, was a new experience for me. He would connect with the audience in very special ways.

Frizzle choked with emotion as he shared the story of an event during a Travis Park worship service decades earlier.

A young woman from the community had been to our group a few times. She had an illegitimate baby and wanted it to be baptized. Dr. Copeland did not want her to be alone when she brought the baby to the altar, so he asked if some of us would come down and stand with her. He baptized the baby and explained that we were friends and how important it is to have people who care. Even to this day I can't get over the care he gave to make sure she was not alone. It was very special.

Brantley soon had Frizzle teaching junior high youth, something that would influence his future career decisions. "I liked that a lot," he said. He stayed in San

Antonio after his military service and went to Trinity University. He got married and taught in San Antonio for a year while his wife finished her studies at Trinity. "I hadn't planned to be a teacher, but I loved it and knew I had found my calling." He and his wife returned to Massachusetts, where he attended graduate school and became a public school counselor, history teacher, assistant superintendent, and superintendent.

Kenneth's interest in music endeared him to people at Travis Park, just as it had in his earlier appointments and teenage years. "He would play the piano at our staff Christmas parties and jazz it up," Janert said. Both Copeland daughters inherited their father's love of music. Patti became an accomplished soprano soloist, Sue an accomplished pianist and organist. The daughters also inherited their father's commitment to the faith. Patti has worked in local churches in the areas of youth work and finance in Texas. Sue has done family counseling related to local churches in the San Antonio area.

Kenneth was president of both the San Antonio Council of Churches and Lions Club, and was a member of the Methodist Hospital board and the Texas Alcohol and Narcotics Education, Inc., executive committee.

While he was president of the downtown Lions Club, the entire membership decided to surprise him by attending worship services at Travis Park. Kenneth was startled when he walked into the sanctuary and saw his fellow members sitting before him, but his ever-present sense of humor did not fail him. Smiling, he said, "You can't imagine what a shock it is for the shepherd to come to see his flock, and to look over the edge of a cliff and see two hundred Lions." The club gave him an academic robe after he received his honorary doctorate from Southwestern University in 1951.

While in San Antonio, Kenneth became friends with Howard Butt Jr., whose parents, Howard and Mary, had moved from Tennessee to the Hill Country of Texas at the turn of the twentieth century. The business they established is one of the nation's largest privately held grocery companies today. Close friends with W. Angie and A. Frank Smith and their wives, the senior Butts established in 1933 one of Texas' earliest foundations for their charitable, educational, and philanthropic concerns. It continues today with the mission of: "Renewal of society through the renewal of the Church; Church renewal through renewal of the family; family renewal through renewed individuals."

Howard Butt Jr. serves as president of the foundation and is a catalyst for bringing together spiritual and lay leaders from all walks of life to share ideas and learn from each other for spiritual renewal and servant leadership. He founded the internationally known Laity Lodge near Kerrville, Texas; it is a unique oasis of spiritual vitality that serves congregations, pastors, writers, businesses, and professionals, as well as others interested in lay leadership.

Butt worked closely with Billy Graham during and just after his college days at Baylor University. Together, with the Southern Baptist Seminary in Louisville, Kentucky, they sponsored Layman's Leadership

Institutes, meetings of prominent business and professional leaders that continued through the 1970s.

Butt preached for Kenneth on several occasions when Kenneth had to be away from his pulpit.

"I remember most Kenneth's personal warmth which came through in his preaching," Butt said. "As an evangelical, he was constructive in his relationship within Methodism and within the broader Christian community, as typified by the fact that he would have a Baptist layman speak from his pulpit."

Butt also remembers Kenneth's "deep commitment to the Scriptures and his feeling that we should be calling people to Christ. That characterized his own preaching, and I'm sure it was why he wanted me to do some preaching for him. We had a deep personal and spiritual resonance."

Despite a heavy schedule of preaching, pastoral work, and counseling, Kenneth found time to write. *A Primer of Beliefs for Methodist Laymen*, produced by Tidings, was released in more than a dozen printings. It was later reissued following the 1968 Methodist-EUB union as a *Primer of Beliefs for United Methodists*. He dedicated the small book to "my Catherine," and it sold more than 100,000 copies.

He wrote a chapter for *My Call to Preach*, a popular book published by the Methodist Board of Education in 1962, and wrote articles in denominational publications, including "The Pastoral Prayer," in *The New Christian Advocate* in 1967, and "Essentials to Evangelism" in *The Upper Room Pulpit*, February 1952.

The years at Travis Park were full of milestones for the Copeland family. Kenneth's beloved parents died: John Wesley in 1956, and Nancy in 1959. Catherine's father, Robert Andrews, died in April 1949, just before their move to San Antonio; her mother, Myrtle Andrews, died in 1956. Patti and Sue finished high school in San Antonio. Patti graduated from Southwestern University in Georgetown in 1955 and married Bill Ard in 1958. Sue attended Southern Methodist University and graduated from Trinity University. She married Preston Dial Jr. in 1959. They were divorced in 1975. She married Peter Callins in 2002.

During his service in San Antonio, Kenneth's reputation grew throughout the South Central Jurisdiction and beyond. He traveled widely to fulfill speaking engagements and served on various boards of churchwide organizations and institutions. He served as a member of the Methodist Board of Evangelism from 1952 to 1960.

The church's U.S. jurisdictional system was created at the 1939 church union. Delegates—half lay and half clergy—from each conference within the jurisdiction gather every four years. A primary task of a jurisdictional conference is to elect new bishops to fill vacancies caused by deaths and retirement and to assign all bishops to area supervision for the next four years.

Being elected a delegate to a general or jurisdictional conference is an honor. Annual Conference lay delegates elect lay delegates to the quadrennial gatherings; clergy elect clergy delegates. In 1948, Kenneth was elected a first reserve delegate to the South Central Jurisdictional Conference. He was the fourth of ten clergy delegates elected to the 1952 General and Jurisdictional Conferences from the Southwest Texas Conference; the second clergy delegate elected in 1956; and the second elected in 1960.

Travis Park Church hosted the 1960 South Central Jurisdictional Conference, an event that was a major turning point for the Copeland family. "Surely this conference will be a historic one and will bring great blessing to all who participate," Kenneth wrote in the June 21 issue of the *Travis Park News*.

Kenneth received a few votes for bishop as early as the 1952 jurisdictional conference. Catherine said that on several previous occasions, Bishop A. Frank Smith had teasingly warned Kenneth that "lightning is going to strike you one of these days." That lightning struck in San Antonio in 1960, as the 316 delegates filled five episcopal vacancies in the jurisdiction. Voting began with delegates writing the names of five clergy persons on blank ballots. The first individual to receive the required sixty percent of the votes was O. Eugene Slater, followed by W. Kenneth Pope, Paul V. Galloway, and Aubrey G. Walton. Kenneth, the last, received 210 votes on the ninth ballot; 190 votes were needed for election.

"The quintet of new bishops were a diverse group, alike chiefly in that all were pastors when elected," wrote Theodore Agnew in his book, *The South Central Jurisdiction 1939–1972: A Brief History and an*

Interpretation. "Copeland, at forty-eight, was the youngest of the five and the first host pastor to be elected, bringing to the episcopacy a matchless pulpit eloquence and the special brand of heart-religion which had characterized the Methodist Protestants. . . ."

Kenneth and Fred G. Holloway were the first former Methodist Protestant clergymen elected bishops after those elected at the 1939 church union. (Holloway was elected at the 1960 Northeastern Jurisdictional Conference.) It would be another twelve years before John B. Warman, the next and last former Methodist Protestant clergyman, would be elected at the Northeastern Jurisdictional Conference.

Kenneth did not lift a finger to be elected bishop, according to Catherine. Nevertheless, he had gained prominence in his own annual conferences in Texas and Oklahoma and throughout the jurisdiction. He was widely known as an effective preacher, pastor, and administrator. Friends throughout the church, including delegates and even bishops, pushed for his election. Posters and campaign speeches were not present as they are today, but there were plenty of hallway conversations.

During the conference, Catherine and Kenneth stayed at the nearby St. Anthony Hotel. Catherine recalls that as they dined alone one evening, Kenneth said, "You know, we haven't talked about this, but it looks like I might be elected bishop. What do you think about it?"

"I responded, 'It isn't what I think about it. What do you think about it?' He replied, 'I've never asked my church for anything, and I'm not asking now. If elected, I will do the very best I can.' He was extremely sincere about that. He would have been very happy to stay at Travis Park," Catherine said. The church had 4,460 members at the time.

More bishops were elected across the church in 1960 than in any year since 1939. Kenneth was the third-youngest bishop elected in American Methodism and the fifth pastor elected from Travis Park. The others were John M. Moore, Edwin D. Mouzon, Arthur J. Moore, and Paul B. Kern. Dan E. Solomon served at Travis Park from 1977 to 1983, and was elected bishop in 1988.

Kenneth was honored to be elected to the church's highest office. But adding to the significance was his consecration on June 26, 1960, at the altar of Travis Park, the church where he had labored and loved, laughed and cried, and felt immeasurable joy and sadness. Undoubtedly, it was also a bittersweet time, as he realized that he would never again serve as pastor of a local congregation.

7

Nebraska

After his election as bishop, Kenneth was assigned to a four-year term in Nebraska, the northernmost state in the jurisdiction. Relocating there was a major adjustment for Kenneth and Catherine. It is not known if Bishop Copeland had ever been in the state, but Catherine had not. They left the familiar support of a loving congregation and moved to a different culture, hundreds of miles from their children and grandchildren. Nebraska winters are notoriously cold. Being a bishop meant much more travel and long periods away from home. Traveling south from Lincoln was difficult, with no trains or nonstop flights to major southern cities such as Dallas.

If the Copelands had any misgivings about moving to Nebraska, they never spoke of them. They quickly discovered that Nebraska's reputation as a cold state was eclipsed by the warmth and hospitality of the Cornhusker Methodists. They soon extolled the virtues of Nebraska and its people. Bishop Copeland had made a personal pledge to do his best wherever the church sent him as bishop, and he would keep that promise. He had a strong commitment to the historic itinerant system of Methodism, a commitment he would expect from clergy under his appointment.

The wives of many bishops, particularly those with children at home, often experienced loneliness as their husbands traveled within the episcopal area and beyond. This was not a problem for Catherine; she accompanied Kenneth to most engagements within the conference and always on trips outside the country. She recalled with regret one trip she didn't attend with him. He had been a bishop for more than a decade and they had been assigned to a new area. "I stayed behind to prepare for an open house scheduled at the parsonage during the upcoming annual conference. When Kenneth came home he told me how lonely it was without me. I felt badly." Her absence was even more poignant in retrospect. This was Kenneth's last meeting with the council before his death.

Alva H. Clark of Omaha, head of the Nebraska delegation to the 1960 Jurisdictional Conference, recalls the dynamics behind Bishop Copeland's assignment to Nebraska.

"As usual in the South Central Jurisdiction, other conferences had worked together and predetermined who was going to come to Nebraska," he said. "They had a particular person in mind for Nebraska, but we didn't want him. I visited with Bishop Copeland and learned he was enthusiastic about coming to

Nebraska, so we mounted a vigorous effort to get him assigned to us."

Clark was a member of the episcopal committee that assigned the bishops. "The chairman of the committee was determined to get his choice sent to Nebraska. When we voted, that wasn't the case, so he called for a prayer meeting. We got on our knees, prayed, and voted again. Same results, so he called for another prayer meeting. After several of these he finally gave up."

If there was culture shock for Bishop Copeland, it was related to evangelism. His approach, including altar calls, was a bit foreign to midwestern religious practices. Methodists were the largest Protestant communion in Nebraska, but Catholics and Lutherans, with more formal worship patterns, greatly influenced the culture.

Nebraska congregations might host preaching missions but rarely did they have revivals. When Billy Graham held a crusade in Omaha in the 1960s, Bishop Copeland was surprised by the lack of enthusiasm and support for the event. He was a supporter of Graham. He and Catherine attended one of his crusades in New York.

Clark, then pastor of St. Paul's Church in Omaha, said he was one of those who was less than enthusiastic about the crusade. "Graham's people came to my church on Sunday morning to hear me preach to see if I was acceptable for referrals from the crusade. I didn't like that. However, I've been appreciative of Billy Graham since, and the fact that he's broadened his spirit."

Bishop Copeland gave a series of lectures at Iliff School of Theology in Denver, and told of a Nebraska clergyman who had expressed concern about Copeland's assignment. The man said a southern bishop would mean a wave of evangelism in Nebraska.

Bishop Copeland said:

> If he meant evangelism, I earnestly and fervently and prayerfully hope his prediction comes to pass. If he meant revivalism, then that probably is open to debate. What is more regrettable, I think, is to know there are some who think of evangelism condescendingly, sometimes even with a sneer, in the same way that some use the word "gospel" in relation to "these cheap gospel songs" as compared to the so-called great music of the church. No, evangelism and revivalism are not twin brothers and are not necessarily bound in the same package, either as to principle or as to pattern. Evangelism is a time-honored word and is as relevant for the program of the church today as the word worship or consecration.

The culture may have been different for the Copelands in Nebraska, but when the bishop preached in local churches and district events across the state, lay men and women responded to his calls for commitment and his invitations to make their desires and intentions known by moving from their pews to the altar.

He was a master communicator with wide experience as a pastor, and knew his audience. He could speak their language and reach their hearts, whether they were a few dozen white ranchers in a small frame church in the western Sandhills or a racially mixed congregation in Omaha's inner city.

Bishop Copeland had a reputation for using the public media to speak to those outside the Methodist constituency, but he didn't neglect communication channels within the church. He wrote a monthly letter for the *Nebraska Area News Edition* of *Together* magazine. Topics included evangelism, education, and stewardship. He occasionally shared a personal event such as, "A Preacher's Birthday," marking his thirty-fifth anniversary as a preacher. He wrote on seasonal topics, particularly Advent and Easter. His letters frequently addressed the church's appointment system of clergy. These messages included the titles "On the Return of Your Pastor," "Our New Minister," "Your New Pastor," "Workers Together," "When Pastors Move," and "The Itinerant Ministry."

There was some speculation about where the Copelands would be assigned at the end of their first four-year term in Nebraska. As the 1964 South Central Jurisdictional Conference in Dallas approached, a Lincoln newspaper carried a prominent story saying that Texans were maneuvering to have the Copelands returned to the Lone Star State. Embarrassed, the Copelands assured Nebraskans they were happy in their present assignment and were not seeking a change. They were reassigned for another four years.

A Roman Catholic bishop, at Bishop Copeland's invitation, addressed a session of the Nebraska Annual Conference for the first time in 1966. Bishop James V. Casey of the Lincoln Diocese spoke of the Vatican

Council, describing it as "representative of a different climate, a step to the unity which we believe Christ wants." Bishop Copeland was a strong supporter of ecumenical relations and worked with councils of churches wherever he served. While not advocating a single super church, he was a strong disciple of oneness in Christ.

Serving in Nebraska provided a special opportunity for Bishop Copeland to become better acquainted with the Evangelical Brethren Church (EUB), which would join the Methodist Church in 1968, becoming the United Methodist Church. Since he had come from the smallest of the denominations that united in 1939, he was especially suited to lead the Methodist-EUB union process with sensitivity.

The Methodist Church had about four hundred congregations in Nebraska; the EUB church had one hundred. In contrast, the entire state of Texas had only seven EUB churches. Even before union, at least sixteen communities in Nebraska had "yoked ministries," where a pastor of one denomination served congregations of both. EUB Bishop Paul W. Milhouse worked with Bishop Copeland to guide the union plans. Milhouse resided in Kansas City and supervised the Southwestern Area of the EUB Church, including Nebraska.

In the spring of 1966, Bishop Copeland gave a personal witness in favor of the Methodist-EUB union during a meeting of the Methodist Council of Bishops in Louisville, Kentucky. He reflected on the 1939 union and called on Methodists and EUBs to see themselves as being drawn together by a common devotion, not driven together by a common danger.

In a remarkable sentence, he summarized the Wesleyan heritage which he said the two groups shared:

> With roots deep in the Wesleyan revival; with a common appreciation for the harmony of knowledge and piety; with a common concern for the world parish; with a common dedication to a personally experienced faith; with a common commitment to Christ as Savior, Lord, Redeemer and Friend; and with a common conviction that this faith should manifest itself in the service of love for Christ through our fellow man; all in the strength and power of the Holy Spirit, we are being drawn together with ties that bind, and there would seem to be little reason for remaining apart.

He said the two groups were drawn together by a common devotion to three basic symbols of ecclesiastical union which they already shared: ministry, membership, and the sacraments.

He also pointed to a common devotion to the evangelistic and social task "to make disciples and spread scriptural holiness throughout the land and throughout the world."

"We do not believe there are any off-limits to the church, no area of human life into which the Gospel cannot go," he said. "We are compelled by divine command to make disciples of all nations, and from this command there is no honorable discharge."

Lastly, he said a common devotion to the "oneness of the body of Christ," drew the two denominations together. "We believe we are already one in his love," he said. "We must be one in our witness to his love."

At the time Kenneth Copeland assumed his role as bishop, the cold war was in full swing, the civil rights movement was reaching a crescendo, America's involvement in Vietnam was deepening, and the U.S. space program was emerging.

Mass media and academic journals were beginning to address a generation gap of major proportions in the United States. It especially grieved Bishop Copeland to hear about the tensions between young and old. He expressed dismay the first time he heard a young girl say, "I hate my mother." He championed the promotion of healthy, Christian families across the entire church.

A front-burner issue during the 1960s was American Methodism's racially segregated Central Jurisdiction, which had been created with the 1939 church union. The Jurisdiction officially ended in 1968, Bishop Copeland's last year in Nebraska.

Three African American congregations in the state merged earlier with the Nebraska conference. Newman Methodist Church of Lincoln transferred into the Nebraska Conference on February 28, 1964, and both Clair Memorial and Union in Omaha transferred on May 19, 1964. Bishop Copeland guided and implemented the merger plan with Bishop Matthew W. Clair Jr., his colleague in the Central West Conference of the Central Jurisdiction. Emmett S. Streeter, pastor at Clair, eventually became the first black district superintendent in the conference.

"No generation has ever stood more in need of a Moses to lead us out of the wilderness of hatred, intolerance, and bigotry into a promised land of God's love and grace," Bishop Copeland said at the uniting service for the two Omaha congregations. "We are drawn together as Christians by a common devotion, and we shall remain together as long as that devotion remains." The bishop's experience in Nebraska, which had a small African American population, prepared him for a greater challenge when he moved to Houston.

Those who knew Bishop Copeland well were aware that adapting to the direct, sometimes blunt manner of the Midwest was initially difficult for him. Bishops in the South were treated with a great deal of deference, protocol, and respect, even fear. As a group, bishops in the Methodist Episcopal Church South did not expect their judgment or leadership to be challenged. Nebraskans showed respect and affection for Bishop Copeland, but never hesitated to disagree with him in a forthright manner. Later in his episcopacy, he expressed appreciation for that characteristic. "There was rarely any game-playing," one of his colleagues observed. "He always knew where he stood."

Regarding Bishop Copeland's leadership style during his years in Nebraska, Alva Clark said, "His ability to avoid being authoritarian came as much from his Methodist Protestant heritage as from anything else." The Methodist Protestant Church had no bishops and thus put a heavy emphasis on lay involvement in decision-making. Clark also praised the leadership provided throughout the conference by Catherine.

The jurisdiction system was problematic for many Nebraskans who felt overlooked and powerless; the region was dominated by much larger southern conferences, particularly those in Texas. The perspectives of Nebraskans on issues such as racial justice and equality sometimes brought them into conflict with members in states such as Louisiana and Arkansas.

On the other hand, Clark said Nebraskans received value from the southern Methodists in such matters as adult education, which he said had not been emphasized as much in the northern branch of Methodism. "So many of us built local church education programs because of these emphases," he said. "They became a strength of Nebraska Methodism."

Because of the numerical strength of conferences in the southern part of the jurisdiction, Nebraskans were unable to have one of their own clergy elected a bishop until 1976. Bishop Copeland appointed Kenneth W. Hicks district superintendent in 1968. Hicks served eight years as bishop in Arkansas, and eight in Kansas. He retired in 1992 and now resides in Little Rock.

"Having Bishop Copeland as our leader was a high point in our episcopal experience in Nebraska," Hicks said. "He enjoyed being a bishop. He didn't take his episcopal responsibilities lightly at all, but he was able to enjoy the fellowship of laity and ministers."

Hicks told of playing golf with the bishop in Norfolk, Nebraska. "I teed off, and the ball went straight up and came down about fifteen feet from where we were standing. Bishop Copeland said, 'Kenneth, I'm glad to know you aren't neglecting your ministry for golf.'"

Golf was an important release for the bishop. Charles W. Williams, a clergyman in the Texas Conference, described him as a better-than-average golfer. "He knew the game and he could talk the game, but like most of us, he could talk it better than he could play it."

Alva Clark was pastor of the large St. Paul's Methodist Church in Omaha and a strong leader in missions and church extension. Under his leadership, the conference launched a program of new church development just before Bishop Copeland's arrival.

"Bishop Copeland was always very cooperative and eager to help us move in that direction," said Clark. "He would take full responsibility to appoint leadership for new churches but gave us the responsibility for planning and putting together the conference programs that made it possible for this development to come."

Clark once drove the bishop to a large grassy field at 120th and Dodge Streets on the western edge of Omaha. "I told him I'd like to build a new church. He said, 'Okay, go ahead.'" With that approval and encouragement, St. Paul's Church had a financial campaign, a third of which was designated for the church budget, a third for a new addition to the church building, and a third to buy ten acres for the new congregation.

Clark praised Bishop Copeland's ability to bridge the gap that sometimes existed between rural and urban congregations and communities in the state. "He helped rural churches see that we needed to move quickly in the urban areas. People were moving from rural churches to the cities, but not identifying with any churches there. This was a major emphasis for Bishop Copeland. He had a great interest in it."

As one might expect, the bishop's leadership in Nebraska included a strong emphasis on evangelism. "It was more than just telling somebody else to go out and make disciples," Clark said. "He went out and helped it happen in local churches. We had no reason to feel that in any part of the state Bishop Copeland was leaving us out there on a limb by ourselves. He was there to support and encourage. I can remember sitting in a car for hours listening to him share his vision for the conference." Clark also recalled that, as a preacher, the bishop was "very contemporary in emphasis, a long way ahead of his time."

Bishop Copeland served as a member of the church's Board of Missions while in Nebraska. Largely because of that involvement, he enabled churches to develop a greater sense of being part of a global mission. "We developed mission projects that extended globally, all of that being done with his encouragement and enthusiasm," Clark recalled.

Bishop Copeland's involvement in the church was not limited to Nebraska or even the United States. Like John Wesley, the world was indeed his parish. He served as an officer of the Methodist Board of Missions and was chairman of the Methodist Board of Christian Social Concerns Division of Peace and World Order. He was a leader in the church's General Committee on Family Life during his second term in Nebraska.

Even in the Council of Bishops, which met twice annually, the bishop's skill as a musician was recognized.

In his book, *History of the Council of Bishops of the United Methodist Church 1939–1979*, Bishop Roy H. Short noted that during his council membership, Bishop Copeland was the assistant pianist to Bishop Earl W. Ledden. Short described Bishop Copeland as being "of medium height and agile in his movements. He was a man of great energy and was forever busy. He had a warm, friendly spirit and always wore a kindly smile. He was good company and was well-liked wherever he went."

At the first Council of Bishops meeting after his election, held in Chicago in November 1960, the episcopal leaders sent a telegram to newly elected President John F. Kennedy, assuring him of their prayers. At his second Council of Bishops meeting in 1961 in Boston, Bishop Copeland was in charge of a devotional service for the bishops at the historic Old North Church. The council voted to place a plaque in the church in honor of Charles Wesley, who had preached there before leaving America in 1736. The plaque was hung several months later.

Bishops were expected to visit Methodist and ecumenical work in countries outside the United States at least once every four years. These trips could be physically challenging. To meet with indigenous church leaders in some isolated locations, Bishop and Mrs. Copeland took primitive modes of transportation over rough terrain.

It was as the Copelands prepared for a trip to Asia that Bishop Copeland received his last letter from Bishop A. Frank Smith. The bishop wished them well on their upcoming episcopal visitation. "We will follow you in our thoughts and in our prayers from day to day," he wrote. "We love you a whole lot at our house and are mighty proud of you. Blessings upon you always." Smith died three days later.

Bishop Copeland was the fraternal messenger from the Methodist Church to United Church of Christ leaders in Japan in October 1961. In 1962, they visited several countries in Southeast Asia, including Singapore, Taiwan, Hong Kong, and Japan. While in Taiwan, the Copelands had tea with the country's first lady, Madame Chiang Kai-shek. She had several connections with Methodism, including a prayer meeting she attended weekly. Madame Chiang later came to Nebraska Wesleyan University in 1966. She spoke to a packed auditorium of students, faculty, and visitors, and received an honorary doctor of humane letters degree.

Bishop Copeland reported on his Asia trip to the Council of Bishops, concluding: "Christ is a world Savior! The Methodist Church is a world church! John Wesley's world parish is our parish, and the fulfillment of Christ's command to go into all the world and make disciples of all nations remains the only alternative to world chaos and destruction. When I see the work of the Methodist Church in southeast Asia, I am proud to be a Methodist!"

In 1979, Catherine shared some of her memories of their travel experiences with a reporter for the *San Antonio Express-News*. "We stayed in places from a Taiwan palace to a dirt-floored hut of a Methodist minister in Borneo with mice scampering about. I managed to thank our hosts even when served snake and raw octopus and when the Chinese served whole boiled chickens with their heads hanging over the bowl edge with the eyes staring at me." She also remembered accepting rice, knowing that her hosts would have to skip a meal, and traveling by Jeep for miles over monsoon-wrecked roads in the Philippines. "We went by riverboat through jungles," she recalled. "Once, a small plane carried us along with a pilot, chickens, produce, and another passenger."

Short described Bishop Copeland's leadership style as careful and democratic in spirit. Copeland's views on the role of a bishop were included in an address he gave at the consecration of four new bishops at the 1972 South Central Jurisdictional Conference in Houston. He urged the new bishops to be symbols and instruments of unity, agents of leadership, and pastors. The latter point was certainly the most evident and prominent characteristic of his own ministry. Above all else, he was a bishop with a pastor's heart.

Bishops, he said, must take unity seriously as a gift of the Holy Spirit. "If we take responsibility for making it real in our relationships with God and with each other as followers of Christ, it can help us to thaw out this 'cold war' between the pietist and the activist, the conservative and the liberal divisions."

The growing tensions in the church between liberals and conservatives were a concern to Bishop Copeland. He frequently addressed the issue in sermons, writings, and lectures. He was, at heart, a reconciler, and divisions in the church pained him.

The bishop affirmed the trend toward more participatory democracy in decision-making processes of the church, and said one cannot be a dictator and a leader at the same time. "One cancels out the other. In fact, I am convinced that the less one drives and the more one leads, the more creative and effective one will be." Quoting Bishop A. Frank Smith, he said, "While the driver sometimes gets the job done quicker, I believe the leader gets the job done better and with more permanence."

In his charge to the new bishops, Bishop Copeland warned them that leadership can be costly, lonely, and vulnerable.

> A leader must be out in the front line of those who are being led. The pulpit is never a bomb-proof shelter from the fiery blasts of the devil. The cabinet room is not a place where, in protective isolation, we make decisions affecting the lives of ministers and their families with cold objectivity which fails to take into account where they hurt and why. The presiding officer's chair in an annual conference is not an exalted throne from which one rules.

A good leader, he added, must be willing to be led. "A leader in the church of Jesus Christ will first of all seek the leadership of God's Holy Spirit and will respond to that leadership with increasing sensitivity and responsibility."

Pastoral responsibilities should always be primary for a bishop, he declared. "If meetings and administrative details cancel out a bishop's responsibility as pastor, persons are hurt and the church is hampered in its progress toward fulfilling the total will of God for its life in the world."

In the March 1966 issue of *The Methodist Woman*, he said, "I consider my responsibilities as a spiritual leader first and as an administrator second. I have a pastor's heart and hope that I can help ministers and laymen see and understand the Christ I know."

He said bishops must above all else be concerned with persons.

> A good pastor is not first of all issue-oriented. He or she is first of all person-oriented. Of course, we must be keenly aware of the issues, alert to their root causes and their effects on the church, the community and the world. However, it is only as we are person-oriented that we can approach the issues with redemptive and reconciling involvement. We can relate to our people if we remember that they are first of all God's people, and they remain his people.

An example of Bishop Copeland's personality and pastoral heart was his visit in April 1967 to Mrs. Karl Aldrich, the oldest Methodist in Nebraska. Aldrich had celebrated her 107th birthday the previous January. The bishop initiated the fifty-mile trip from Lincoln to Brock, where Aldrich resided with her daughter. Because she had difficulty hearing, Bishop Copeland sat close as he asked questions about her life and faith. He sang "Rock of Ages" for her when he learned it was her favorite hymn. A few months later, twelve hundred Nebraska Methodists gathered in Lincoln during the regular annual conference sessions for a gala banquet celebrating Nebraska's centennial. Aldrich was an honored guest at the head table; Bishop Copeland presented her with a centennial medallion.

An example of Bishop Copeland's pastoral style of administration is found in a presentation he made at a large congregation in Nebraska that was experiencing serious tension between pastor and some members. He began by reading Ephesians 5:1–21 from the New English Bible, and explained that he came at the invitation of the church's board chairman.

> Under the structure of The Methodist Church, I come as chief pastor, and, therefore, my message is a pastoral one. I speak in love, as I am compelled to speak honestly and sincerely. In this message I call for repentance, reconciliation, and restoration of the unity of the faith in the bond of peace.
>
> For several months, this church has suffered unnecessary and, at times, unbearable pains. Any diagnosis in depth leaves no room for naïve optimism nor, certainly, self-defeating pessimism. An honest appraisal, however, would bring us to face reality and confess that all too much time and energy have been spent on personal defensiveness and blaming others . . . and only God knows how many people have looked to the church for bread only to be given a stone.

Lamenting the "wall" that existed between the pastor and some members, he said, " . . . let me make clear that I do not come here to assess blame or invoke penalty or judge the degree of guilt. I come simply to echo the cry which comes from the heart of the church when any part of the body falls ill."

He challenged the pastor and congregation to "get down to the business of being the church. . . . A sanctuary needs to be built. World Service and Advance Specials need to grow. A spiritual solution must be found to a war in Vietnam, but we can be of little value to others if we cannot find peace in our own group."

In a closing challenge, he urged his audience to recognize their past mistakes and, by God's grace, to correct them.

> The future is before us; Christ is before us. In fact, Christ is with us, and he calls us to follow him. I commit myself to greater diligence to seek his will in prayer, to understand his word through the Bible and the revelations of the Holy Spirit, to preach a Christ-centered Gospel to today's world, and to seek to spread his redemptive love with whom it is my privilege to share. Will you join me in this commitment? Somehow I believe you will and may God be praised.

Church-related institutions received strong support from Bishop Copeland, who served on the board of trustees of several colleges during his lifetime. Nebraska had several hospitals, retirement homes, schools of nursing, and camps. He particularly enjoyed his relationship with leaders at Nebraska Wesleyan University, which was located just one block from his office. He was a member of the governing board at the school, which gave him an honorary doctor of sacred theology degree in 1961. In his first address to the faculty, during a time when there was considerable unrest on American campuses, he spoke on "Academic Freedom and Christian Responsibility."

> We do not speak of church and college as separate institutions. Neither do we speak of the Church as some force outside the college imposing its rule and authority onto the college.
>
> We believe the Church to be the body of Christ in the world, and the particular segment of that body which we call the Methodist Church looks upon all its institutions as children who seek to fulfill its life and purpose within society. Therefore, we here in Nebraska Wesleyan University are as much a part of the Church as the preachers who grace our pulpits each Sunday.

Bishop Copeland affirmed both academic freedom for the college and freedom of the pulpit for the preachers, but said that, in both cases, "I cannot possibly conceive of any frame of reference within which such freedom could possibly operate to the good of mankind except within the context of Christian responsibility."

Academic freedom, from a Christian point of view, is more concerned with the persons being taught than the subject matter being presented, he continued.

> After all, we do not teach lessons; we teach persons. This is not to suggest we disregard the truth revealed in the pages comprising the lessons. On the contrary! We will be more concerned with discovering the truth when we remember it is to be communicated to persons whose lives will be affected for good or for ill. . . . Truth, in its largest context, takes into account what happens

to these persons as much as the facts being presented to them.

Academic freedom, he said, is accountable ultimately to God. "The Christian Church affirms truth and Jesus Christ as inseparable. It affirms that truth is not, after all, a theory, but comes to life in a person. And the Church believes that the person in whom truth came to life fully was Jesus the Christ . . . The Church believes that wherever you find truth you also find the footprints of Jesus the Christ."

In closing, he said, "Academic freedom within Christian responsibility demands we give God a hearing, truth a chance, and conscience a voice."

Bishop Copeland's time in Nebraska was a turbulent period for the nation, marked by the assassinations of President John F. Kennedy in 1963, and both Dr. Martin Luther King Jr. and Senator Robert Kennedy in 1968.

King had been the guest speaker for the eighth quadrennial meeting of the national Methodist Student Movement in Lincoln during the Christmas holidays of 1964, his first major appearance since receiving the Nobel Peace Prize. Bishop Copeland spoke at Nebraska Wesleyan soon after King's death and praised the civil rights leader's dedication to the proposition that "all men are created equal and endowed by their Creator with certain unalienable rights, among which are life, liberty, and the pursuit of happiness."

"It remains for us who live on in the struggle to be solemnly dedicated to the human dignity which we believe to be given to all mankind by our God to be enjoyed in this life," Bishop Copeland said. "When we

97

can reach that day of fulfillment of liberty and justice for all, then we can declare the Rev. Dr. Martin Luther King Jr. not victim, but victor. So help us God."

In a 1968 address, Bishop Copeland spoke of the temptation to retreat into the past when faced with the complexities of the present. "I have lived in two—principally two—ministerial generations," he said. "I was born in a Methodist parsonage. I saw the generation of my father and then I've tried to see my own, and I must say to you that there are many times I'd like to retreat into the relative security of the ministerial world my father knew."

He said he enjoyed the popular *Gunsmoke* television series because:

> The issues are all black and white, and there are good guys and there are bad guys. The bad guys always get it and the good guys, they always come out on top. It's a lot easier for me to identify with Matt Dillon as he pounds the teeth out of some drunken cowpoke in the Long Branch Saloon than it is for me to confront one of my preachers who doesn't like what I've just done.
>
> I confess to you it's a lot easier to do that than to go to general conference and hear them criticizing the bishops. But I have sense enough to know that I can't live in Matt Dillon's world. I have sense enough to know that Matt Dillon's world doesn't exist anymore . . . Oh, I love to sing with you, "America, America, thine alabaster cities gleam undimmed by human tears," but that is not so tonight. I pray that it may be so some day. But America's alabaster cities are not undimmed by human tears.

He challenged his listeners to "go into today's world, the only world we've got," and assured them they would not face the overwhelming challenges alone. "The command is to go into today's world today, not tomorrow, but today. But the command had a condition on it: 'Lo, I am with you always, even unto the end of the world.' He meant precisely that. Thank God, he meant precisely that."

Bishop Copeland rarely showed impatience or irritability, except with ministers who fell short of their capabilities. Catherine recalled the wife of a minister coming to the episcopal residence soon after the close of an annual conference session. "She blessed Kenneth out in no uncertain terms because of what she considered an unworthy appointment for her husband. Kenneth listened patiently and treated her courteously. After she left, he said he couldn't tell her that she was the reason her husband hadn't received a better appointment."

During his second four-year-term in Nebraska, Bishop Copeland represented the Methodist Church at the General Conference of the Methodist Church of Mexico. In August 1966, he, Catherine, and two hundred other Methodists from the state attended the eleventh World Methodist Conference in London. During free time at the conference, Bishop Copeland visited historic sites. He stood in the pulpit at Wesley's Chapel where John and Charles had preached, and played Charles Wesley's organ in the family home next door.

Late in 1967, he and Mrs. Copeland toured Asia for three months, visiting Methodist work in Korea, Japan, Taiwan, Okinawa, Hong Kong, the Philippines, Thailand, India, and Pakistan.

The Nebraska Conference had made a significant financial contribution to new church development in Korea. Finis and Shirley Jeffery, who retired in San Antonio after thirty years as missionaries in Korea, took the Copelands to the mushrooming industrial community of Ulsan in 1967. Finis said Bishop Copeland came not simply as a tourist, but as one interested in the growth and outreach of the Korean Methodist Church. "He asked me to show him a church in an expanding area, so we drove about thirty miles to Ulsan, located in a strategically important area designated for future growth. The Zion Methodist Church in Ulsan had bought a small piece of land and built a church which held about eighteen people. It soon was dwarfed by new apartment buildings."

Finis pointed to a large vacant area across the main road which ran through the center of the town, and told Bishop Copeland the land could be purchased for $4,500. A few months later, as the Copelands prepared to leave Nebraska, they received a love offering of $8,500 from Methodists across the state. They gave the money to new church development in Ulsan. Finis said $4,500 of the gift helped purchase land. The remaining $4,000 was used to construct a dual-purpose building which served as a church on weekends and kindergarten during the week.

Ulsan quickly became an industrial center and today is the primary location for manufacturing the popular Hyundai automobiles. As the congregation grew, it built a large sanctuary and two other buildings used for Christian education, youth activities, and a home for the pastor. The tiny congregation of eighteen people that existed when the Copelands visited in 1967 is now the Ulsan Central Methodist Church with more than seven thousand members. The congregation has helped start several other pioneer churches which are part of a district of twenty-seven Methodist churches. The Central Methodist property in Ulsan, a city of more than five hundred thousand citizens, is valued at more than $2 million.

"God has blessed that love gift, so generously given in faith by Kenneth and Catherine Copeland, far beyond anything we could have imagined," said Finis. "The Korean Methodist Church has been bountifully blessed in the following years."

Bishop Copeland's work on behalf of world missions and peace was recognized in 1967 when the Nebraska Conference Women's Society of Christian Service commissioned a statue in his honor at the new Church Center for the United Nations. Displayed in the eleventh-floor lobby, the *Prince of Peace* sculpture of Christ on a donkey is based on Isaiah 9:6: "For unto us a child is born . . . the Prince of Peace . . ."

The statue was created by Moissaye Marans, a recipient of the Herbert Adams Memorial Award of the

National Sculpture Society who is acclaimed for his work, including an Isaiah statue, *Swords into Ploughshare*. The sculptor's credo was, "Human creative efforts are but a cosmic reflection testifying to the presence of a Supreme Creator who made and regulates the universe." Marans and the Copelands attended the presentation ceremony in New York on April 16, 1967.

The Nebraska women also furnished a small lounge on the eleventh floor in honor of Bishop Copeland. Instead of being named after the honoree, as is the case for other rooms on the floor, it was named, at his request, the Peace Room. Mia Adjali, a longtime staff member at the center, said the Peace Room is a popular place for staff today. "We see it as our room—to rest, eat, and gather for special occasions such as birthdays, or to watch breaking news on television. We also use it for guests when we wish a cozier atmosphere than our offices."

Bishop Copeland's "My Creed for Peace" received wide attention during the time he led the Division of Peace and World Order of the church's Board of Christian Social Concerns. In the creed, he rejected:

- the doctrine of the inevitability of war;
- the inevitability of hunger, poverty, disease, ignorance, superstition, and fear;
- the right of any person to exploit another;
- isolationism;
- the implication that to be loyal to my own country means it impossible for me to have concern for the rest of the world;

- Communism as a workable way of life or a reasonable philosophy of life;
- the assumption that any effort on the part of the church to work for social justice, freedom, brotherhood, and peace is to be condemned as giving aid to Communism;
- the authoritarian demands of the extreme right and those of the extreme left; and
- "suicide or surrender" as the only alternatives in the dilemma which has the world imprisoned.

In contrast, he affirmed:

- peace is the will of God;
- my personal responsibility for peace;
- peace is possible;
- it is necessary to use spiritual armaments in our warfare against spiritual foes and in our crusade for peace;
- the church's place in this crusade, in this effort to transform the instruments of war into the implements of peace;
- the power of light over darkness; and
- my faith in Jesus Christ.

At the end of the creed, he stated his refusal to "surrender to the apostles of darkness, doubt, degradation, and despair," and proclaimed: "I believe the Prince of Peace still lives."

As the bishop reached the end of his eight years in Nebraska, public opinion was turning decisively against U.S. involvement in Vietnam. At a press conference in March 1968, he released the contents of a letter he had sent to President Lyndon B. Johnson, asking him to implement the call from the United Nations

Secretary General to stop bombing in North Vietnam and initiate peace negotiations.

"In a thermonuclear age it seems increasingly clear that a military victory in Vietnam, with any permanent bases for peace, is impossible," Bishop Copeland wrote the president.

While supporting the right of the South Vietnamese to choose their own government, and rejecting the "ideologies of godless Communism," he told President Johnson: "It seems clear that it is to their [the Communists'] advantage to prolong the war at the expense of American lives and American unity. The greatest victory over Communism would be the cessation of hostilities and the preservation of human life and the rehabilitation of South Vietnam."

The bishop would not see peace in Vietnam during his lifetime. Despite peace agreements in 1973, the war continued to escalate. North Vietnam's successful offensive in 1975 resulted in South Vietnam's collapse and the unification of Vietnam by the North.

8

Twin Passions

From an early age, Kenneth Copeland's passions were evangelism and preaching.

His lifetime commitment to evangelism was noted by Kenneth Shamblin in the *1974 Texas Conference Journal*: "He did not set aside a week or a month in a year in which evangelism was to be emphasized. He felt he should be an evangel at all times."

Bishop Copeland's deep and contagious faith was best expressed in his personal life and his preaching ministry, Shamblin said. "He loved being a preacher of God's grace and he brought his richest talent and deepest dedication to this holy ministry."

His effectiveness as a preacher was evident as a youngster and acclaimed as an adult. Page Thomas, director of the Center for Methodist Studies at Southern Methodist University's Bridwell Library, has described the bishop as "One of the greatest preachers the Methodist Church produced this century."

Asbury Lenox was serving as pastor of Memorial Drive United Methodist Church in Houston when Bishop Copeland appointed him superintendent of the Houston North District. "Bishop Copeland took time, not only with superintendents but with pastors, helping them be better preachers and better persons," Lenox said. "I remember him spending hours and hours at a retreat working with two or three preachers at a time on how to preach. He knew how to craft a sermon to reach people and get a response. He made preachers want to do likewise."

While he had served as pastor of one of the denomination's largest congregations, Bishop Copeland warned against confusing bigness with greatness. In an article titled, "A New Year's Wish For My Church," written for *The Methodist Woman* magazine, he disagreed with those who said no church should have more than a thousand members.

> It becomes a tragedy when we think of greatness in terms of bigness . . . Obviously a large church may be a great church, but a small church might be a great church also. However, neither should measure its greatness in terms of statistics, but in terms of dedication, humility, and breadth of love for and service to mankind. Greatness has to do with the extent of our commitment to Christ and the Christian witness. A great church is thoroughly Christian in its theology, its practice and extension of its redemptive love.

James Foster, the current provost for the Texas Conference, was entering ministry when Bishop

Copeland was assigned to the Houston Area. "His love of evangelism and preaching impressed me," Foster said. "Those were two outstanding gifts he brought to the conference. You can mark the beginning of growth again in our conference by his coming to be our bishop." He also praised the bishop's gentle leadership style. Foster was at the Lakeview Conference Center on several occasions when Bishop Copeland preached. "I remember wishing I might preach as well as he did. He had a real gift of sharing the Gospel."

In an article he wrote for *The Upper Room Pulpit* in February 1952, the bishop provided a concise summary of essentials he considered necessary for effective evangelism. Declaring evangelism to be the primary task of the Church, he said the commission Jesus left with his disciples—commanding them to go into the world—cannot be viewed by the modern disciple as an elective. He warned against anything in the church that hinders or subordinates that commission. "The church cannot afford to become bogged down in trivialities while a spiritually hungry world starves for the meat of the Gospel and the sheep for whom Christ died remain lost in the wilderness," he wrote.

Winning souls is difficult, he said, and requires desire and discipline preceded by prayer and preparation. "To do this work effectively and efficiently it becomes apparent, even to the casual observer, that there are certain essentials that cannot be overlooked." Then, in typical Copeland alliterative form, he identified three: "We need convictions that command us, a compassion that compels us, and a consecration that conditions us."

A church member without basic convictions will not give evangelism a second thought, he observed. "A divine conviction is not a neatly formulated theory; it is an eternal truth that will not let one go. It is more than a simple opinion. While an opinion is an idea one holds about certain things, a conviction is a truth that holds the individual."

Effective evangelism cannot have any question marks around Jesus Christ, he said.

> As to his person, his purpose, and his power, there can be no doubts. He is more than a signpost to a way of life; he is life. He is more than a teacher of truth; he is truth. He does more than point out the way; he has become for us the way. When he looks straight into your soul and asks, as he did in the long ago, "Whom say ye that I am?" you must make your own reply. As for me, I join Peter in humbly but sincerely replying, "Thou art the Christ, the Son of the living God." I stand beside Thomas to declare, "My Lord and my God." I will lift my soul in praise with Handel's Messiah and sing with all my soul, "The Lord God omnipotent reigneth."

Reflecting his pastoral spirit, Bishop Copeland called for a compelling compassion, meaning "the capacity to care, carry, and cure."

"Does it matter to us that men are falling all about us every day?" he asked. "Compassion . . . means getting out onto the road of life where people walk with their burdens, fall with their loads, bleed with their wounds, and suffer with their sins."

While evangelism must begin at home, it cannot stay at home, he declared. "We will not overlook our neighbor next door . . . but the commission of Christ included the whole world, and we cannot afford to rest or relax until it has become our parish."

Before going into all the world, he said, evangelists need a consecration that conditions them. This consecration, he elaborated, begins with cleansing. "Over and over again the evangelist must pray his prayer of forgiveness."

Listening for God's instructions is critical, he added. "If Jesus found it necessary during his earthly ministry to go apart for prayer often, how much more must the contemporary disciple of our Lord find it necessary to be alone with God . . . Only as we listen to the voice of God can we then speak as the voice of God."

Bishop Copeland's perspectives on evangelism and preaching were included in a series of lectures he gave at Iliff School of Theology in Denver when he was bishop in Nebraska. Every preacher is under command to do the work of an evangelist, he declared. "To fail to do so is to fail in one of the predominant demands of the Christian minister."

Evangelism should not be limited to or bound by the words used to describe various patterns of evangelism, he said. "Neither are we wise to reject evangelism because we may reject some particular pattern suggested by the boards of the church or our ecclesiastical leaders. Let us never forget that patterns are not sacred; principles are. Patterns change with the changing times; principles never change."

In his Iliff lectures, the bishop gave a one-sentence definition of evangelism as "the presentation of the Christian Gospel in a witness that is both real and relevant, and at the same time redemptive, which contains an invitation from Christ and endeavors to lead the individual to a personal response to the invitation that will result in a decision to accept Jesus Christ as Savior and Lord."

He defined evangelistic preaching as "the pulpit presentation of the Gospel of Jesus Christ in sermonic patterns as an active witnessing designed to bring men to accept Jesus Christ as Savior and commit their lives to him as Lord."

Emphasizing the importance of the Holy Scriptures, he said, "The preacher whose faith finds no roots there will certainly not produce fruits anywhere . . . We had better be sure as we plead with men to accept Jesus Christ as Savior that we are pleading in the name of the God whose face we see in the face of Jesus Christ, revealed clearly in the pages of the Holy Scriptures."

Bishop Copeland embodied a remarkable ability to care for people and to identify with their joys and hurts. That passion, he said, is required of every evangelistic preacher.

> Our caring for people, or our not caring for people, will soon become apparent in our preaching, and especially in any attempt to do evangelistic preaching . . . One has literally no frame of reference for loving and caring for others except as he loves God and knows God loves all mankind. However, the reverse can also be said: when one truly learns to love God sincerely, he will love God's

creatures also. To say, "I love God," and at the same time not love our fellow men is to speak the impossible.

Bishop Copeland was widely known for his ability to craft sermons that resulted in a response from his listeners. In his Iliff lectures, he described that desired response as "man's response to God's grace, man's decision to accept God's grace in Christ." Although the New Testament uses the picture of physical birth to illustrate the redemptive process in the hearts of people, he said there is one significant difference. "An infant has no consent to its being born physically," he said. "A sinner must consent to a spiritual birth. He does not produce it, but he must consent to it . . . The evangelistic preacher must believe this is the ultimate goal in his preaching and with all of his heart and mind he must drive toward this goal in his preaching."

He called on preachers to present the Gospel in such a way as to help create a desire on the part of the listener to accept Christ and consent to his entering the human heart. "It is God's grace that not only forgives us our sins but cleanses our sin, not only does something with the symptoms but roots out the malady, not only controls the practice but does something with the principle. It is God's work in man's heart. The new birth is the creative act of the Holy Spirit whereby the child of darkness is born into a family of God and made a child of light."

Individuals should have an opportunity to make this consent in their own minds and hearts and to make it known every time a sermon is preached,

Bishop Copeland believed. "Some opportunity must be given for the operation of the Holy Spirit in the life of the listener."

"I love the altar call," he declared. "I think it might have been used unwisely at times, but I am sure that it can be used wisely and well and successfully." He suggested various types of invitations but focused on the critical importance of one: a call for sinners to repent of their sins and accept Jesus Christ as Savior and Lord.

> Whether individuals stand or kneel may not need to be debated but the fact that they come forward in the presence of the church and make their declaration is tremendously important. They do not have to do it, of course. One can accept Christ alone. But let me point out the fact that while the New Testament has much to say about personal religion, it has nothing to say about strictly private religion. We are called again and again to confess him before men, and this is a good time to make that initial step.

He stressed the importance of proper follow-up by the pastor and congregation when an individual makes a decision for Christ.

> One of the reasons why we are dropping so many names from the church rolls . . . is because we have not done a good job of assimilating, of following up, of training our people in the Kingdom.
>
> Our task is laid out for us. Both the gateway and the goal are clearly set. Christ is the gateway; consent to Christ is the goal. Let the evangelistic preacher always enter at this gateway and let him travel the road which is

Kenneth was the sixth of ten children born to John Wesley Copeland, a farmer and Methodist preacher, and Nancy (Hively) Copeland.

Kenneth's father was unquestionably the greatest influence on his early life. "I saw in him a Christian mastery of life and felt in his love for me the security of life," he said.

"From my earliest recollection I had a burning desire to preach," Kenneth said.

Of his call to preach at age fourteen, Kenneth said, "There came to my heart the clearest possible revelation that God had laid his hand upon me and wanted me to preach his glorious Gospel."

Kenneth was pastor of the 1,851-member First United Methodist Church in Stillwater, Oklahoma, from 1944 to 1949.

Three former Methodists Protestants at the altar of First United Methodist Church in Stillwater, Oklahoma: (from left) Kenneth Copeland, who led his Texas Conference into Methodist Union in 1939; John Calvin Broomfield, the second Methodist Protestant clergyman elected a bishop in 1939; and Lamar Cooper, Kenneth's closest friend who was, at this time, director of the Wesley Foundation at Oklahoma A&M in Stillwater.

Travis Park United Methodist Church, under reconstruction after a devastating fire in the early hours of October 21, 1955. The project took almost three years and cost $1.5 million.

Music was of special importance to Kenneth from his early childhood; he enjoyed singing and playing the piano, organ, and other instruments. Here, in 1950 at their parsonage home in San Antonio, he sings with daughters Sue (left) and Patti as Catherine plays the piano.

Kenneth Copeland (center, kneeling) was consecrated as a bishop of The Methodist Church on June 26, 1960, at the altar of Travis Park Methodist Church in San Antonio, Texas, where he had served as pastor for twelve years. He was the fifth and final bishop elected at the eight-state South Central Jurisdictional Conference, which was held at Travis Park. Participants in the service included (from left): Donald Redmond, Maggart B. Howell, Bishop William C. Martin, Bishop Paul Martin, Bishop Eugene M. Frank, and Bishop A. Frank Smith.

Present for Kenneth's consecration as bishop in 1960 were four of his brothers. Clockwise, from bottom right: Otto, Kenneth, Cleve, Buck, and Bill.

Newly consecrated Bishop Kenneth W. Copeland with his wife, Catherine, and their daughters Sue and Patti.

Kenneth was a self-taught musician who enjoyed playing the piano at home, for worship services, and at meetings of the Council of Bishops.

Bishop and Mrs. Copeland in one of several reception lines in Nebraska following his assignment there in 1960.

Bishop Copeland (right), in 1964, with longtime friend and mentor Bishop W. Angie Smith.

Bishop Copeland with Madame Chiang Kai-shek in 1966 at Nebraska Wesleyan University in Lincoln where she was given an honorary doctor of humane letters degree. Bishop and Mrs. Copeland had met Madame Chiang four years earlier during their tour of several countries in Southeast Asia.

Late in 1967, Bishop and Mrs. Copeland visited Methodist work in Korea and other Asian countries. Mrs. Copeland is wearing a hanbok made for her by the women in Pusan. When the Copelands left Nebraska in 1968, they received a love offering from Methodists across the state, which they in turn gave to help purchase land and build a new church in Ulsan, Korea. That congregation today has more than seven thousand members.

Bishop and Mrs. Copeland (center) at the 1964 Methodist General Conference in Pittsburgh with Bishop James H. Straughn, left, age 86; and Bishop Herbert Welch, age 102. Straughn was the first clergyman of the former Methodist Protestant Church to be elected a bishop at the time of church union in 1939. Welch, elected a bishop in the Methodist Episcopal Church in 1916, died in 1969 at the age of 107. Welch was the primary author of the widely used Korean Creed found in today's United Methodist Hymnal.

Recognized for his skills as a presiding officer, Bishop Copeland was tapped to lead a business session at the 1968 General Conference in Dallas (pictured here) and at his last General Conference, held in Atlanta in 1972. He gave a memorial address at the 1968 conference, where the Methodist and Evangelical United Bretheren Church formally merged to form the United Methodist Church.

While attending the 1966 World Methodist Conference in London, Bishop Copeland visited Wesley's Chapel and stood in the historic pulpit where John Wesley, Methodism's founder, preached in the eighteenth century.

Bishop Copeland played Charles Wesley's organ in the Wesley House next to Wesley's Chapel on City Road. It was in this house that John Wesley died in 1791.

Kenneth Copeland's election as bishop meant he would never again be the shepherd of a particular congregation, but he never lost his pastoral spirit. In 1967, he visited Mrs. Karl Aldrich, the oldest Methodist in Nebraska, a few months after her 107th birthday. Learning that "Rock of Ages" was her favorite hymn, Bishop Copeland sang it for her.

Bishop Copeland with two leaders of the historically black Gulf Coast Conference who continued in leadership roles with the newly integrated Texas Annual Conference: Richard H. Robinson (left) and W. B. Randolph. Robinson served as pastor, district superintendent, and conference council staff member. Randolph became the first African American superintendent in the new conference.

Robert E. Hayes Sr. served for two years as administrative assistant to Bishop Copeland after his assignment to the Houston Area in 1968. Hayes, who became president of Wiley College in Marshall, Texas, in 1971, was a key figure in the harmonious merger of the historically black and white conferences of the Houston Area into one Texas Annual Conference. Hayes's son, Robert E. Hayes Jr., was elected a bishop in 2004 and serves the Oklahoma Area.

The 1969–70 cabinet of the Gulf Coast Annual Conference (from left): Houston District Superintendent W. B. Randolph; Navasota District Superintendent L. B. Allen; Bishop Copeland; Beaumont District Superintendent C. K. Hayes; and Marshall District Superintendent Phylemon Titus.

Ever a pastor at heart, Bishop Kenneth W. Copeland's compassion and personal warmth are captured in this official portrait.

sometimes long and arduous with those whom he serves, and let him always keep in mind the goal and seek to lead his people to it. This is evangelistic preaching. God help us to do it with dedication.

Throughout his years in Nebraska, Bishop Copeland was in increasing demand as a speaker across the nation. He preached at annual conference sessions, gave lectures on college campuses, and addressed major national gatherings. His speaking schedule for a three-month period in 1968 was typical:

- March 12: 25th anniversary meeting of the San Antonio Chamber of Commerce
- March 31–April 2: a series of six C. I. Jones Lectures at Rayne Memorial Methodist Church in New Orleans
- April 21: Sunday morning worship at Walnut Hill Methodist Church in Dallas
- April 25: the Memorial Service sermon during General Conference in Dallas
- April 28: Sunday morning worship at Highland Park Methodist Church in Dallas
- May 22–24: three Beeson Lectures at the Central Kansas Conference.

A few days later he presided over sessions of his own Nebraska Conference where Methodist-EUB union was approved.

He spoke at the two largest gatherings of Methodist lay people held every four years. Speaking to five thousand Methodist men gathered for their quad-rennnial convocation at Purdue University in 1965, the bishop said it is not enough to share what one thinks about Christ. "We are called upon as Christians to tell what we have come to know about Christ through experience and to share that experience with others.

"We do not bear witness to a certain brand of politics or to a certain philosophy of government or social progress," he continued. "We bear witness to Christ in all kinds of political situations and social problems." Declaring that there are no off limits to the Gospel, he said, "Jesus did not seclude himself in a house by the side of the road in an attempt to be a friend to man. He was found out in the road where men sweat and swear, where they bleed and burn, where they live and love, and where they suffer and serve—and die. And so must the Christian witness."

Bishop Copeland often used alliteration to help his listeners grasp and retain his message. Such was the case when he spoke to several thousand in May 1966 at the quadrennial Women's Assembly in Portland, Oregon.

I sincerely believe the great demand of this generation is the Christian demand to follow Christ! The great discovery of this generation will be the discovery of the lordship of Christ. The great decision of this generation will be the decision to follow Christ, wherever he takes us.

The demand is already with us. The discovery and the decision are ours to make, aided by his Holy Spirit, and make them, we must, if our world is to know either sanity or salvation.

At the close of the 1968 South Central Jurisdictional Conference in Oklahoma City, Bishop Copeland was assigned to the Houston Area with supervision of the white Texas Conference and the black Gulf Coast Conference.

Under the Methodist-EUB 1968 plan of union, each of the five bishops of the former Central Jurisdiction was assigned to a geographic jurisdiction. Bishop Noah W. Moore was assigned to the South Central Jurisdiction and was appointed to the Nebraska Conference to succeed Bishop Copeland. A similar arrangement was made in the new church for seven former EUB bishops.

After eight years in Nebraska, some major adjustments would be necessary for Bishop and Mrs. Copeland. He would be moving from leadership of one of the smallest episcopal areas in the jurisdiction, with 153,000 members, to the largest, with two conferences and a combined membership of 252,000. Waiting for him in Houston was the challenge to create a new multiracial Texas Annual Conference. He had to fairly and equitably combine members and churches from two United Methodist conferences that had long shared common geographic boundaries and a common heritage, but had long been separated by race.

9

Houston

T hus it was that one of Bishop Copeland's most significant achievements during his five years in the Houston Area was the harmonious merger of the 19,000-member black Gulf Coast Conference and the 233,000-member white Texas Conference.

Although Bishop Copeland had helped guide the merger of Nebraska's three black congregations into the predominantly white conference, his challenge was greater in Houston because of southern culture and the larger number of black members and churches. He guided the process with sensitivity and fairness, in a time when racial tensions were high in the church and nation.

Bishop Copeland presided over only one session of the two conferences before they merged to form the new Texas Annual Conference in 1970. Both black and white conferences were earlier known as Texas Conference, but when the Central Jurisdiction was eliminated, the black conference took the name Gulf Coast.

The *Historical Pictorial Souvenir Book* of the black conference was produced in 1984, the bicentennial year of American Methodism. Offering his perspective as an African American, Richard H. Robinson recalled those final Gulf Coast sessions held at Trinity East United Methodist Church in Houston:

> In the 104 years of the Texas Annual Conference, no bishop was called upon to face up to a challenge comparable to the challenge Bishop Copeland faced in May 1969. The issues were never as binding, never as demanding, never more serious. There was so much to be guarded; yet, the demand of "now" called to us to move into new, untrod paths.
>
> Bishop Copeland was a strong and committed leader with basic ideas regarding his relationship to people. All spoke who wanted to speak. All who spoke were heard; yet, never once did we get lost from the path leading to the goal.
>
> Bishop Copeland held forth the attitude of a mature Christian, he remained alert, he kept the total issue in focus, and because of his ability to preside with complete control of the conference an affirmative vote for merger was unanimous.

Serving a short time with Bishop Copeland as the last superintendents of the Gulf Coast Conference were W. B. Randolph, L. B. Allen, C. K. Hayes, and Phylemon Titus. Randolph became the first African American superintendent appointed by Bishop Copeland to the cabinet of the new conference.

A formal service creating the new conference was held in June 1970 at Jones Hall in Houston. Bishop

Copeland presided, but was assisted by former Central Jurisdiction Bishop Willis J. King and South Central Jurisdiction Bishop Paul E. Martin. Bishop Earl G. Hunt Jr., then leader of the Western North Carolina Conference of the Southeastern Jurisdiction, preached the sermon.

In June 1973, just weeks before his death, Bishop Copeland was cited during sessions of the Texas Annual Conference for his leadership on minority concerns and issues, particularly the merger of the two conferences. Clayton E. Hammond, associate executive secretary of the churchwide Commission on Religion and Race, located in Washington, D.C., said that under Bishop Copeland's leadership, the new Texas Conference represented one of the most effective conferences in the United Methodist Church. There had been a "tremendous show of equality and openness, as well as real meaningful signs that this conference is moving into an area of total inclusiveness for all people," he said.

Hammond retired in 1992 and now resides in Los Angeles. He said there was tremendous leadership among the bishops during the 1970s.

> One of the stories we have not told well, and a story that needs to be told, is the witness that Methodists have made to Christendom all over the world on the matter of becoming inclusive. No church has mixed people as well and as justly as the United Methodist Church. I was a critic in those days, but we were working and, thank God, I've lived long enough to see the changes take place.

Since the merger, the Texas Conference has had cross-racial pastoral appointments, black district superintendents, and conference staff members. Robert Hayes Jr., a former treasurer of the Texas Conference, was elected a bishop in 2004 and assigned to the Oklahoma Area. Windsor Village United Methodist Church, a predominantly black church in Houston, is the largest congregation in the entire denomination with 15,500 members. The conference also produced several African American leaders who assumed churchwide responsibilities, including Allen M. Mayes, a longtime staff member of the denomination's Board of Pensions, and Isaac Bivens, staff member of the Methodist Board of Missions.

Alfred L. Norris served as the first African American bishop of the Texas Conference from 2000 until his retirement in 2004. He was the third African American elected a bishop in the South Central Jurisdiction. He was elected in 1992 and served the Northwest Texas–New Mexico Area for eight years before moving to Houston.

When the 1974 Texas Annual Conference sessions were held a few months after Bishop Copeland's death, he was commended for "giving himself unreservedly to the needs and desires of both black and white persons" and for having love that "was not limited to any color but was shed alike upon all people." J. Kenneth Shamblin, pastor of the large white St. Luke's United Methodist Church in Houston, gave the tribute. [Shamblin would be elected a bishop at the next jurisdictional conference in 1976.]

HOUSTON

An editorial in the *Tyler Morning Telegraph* in August 1973 praised Bishop Copeland's leadership, particularly in uniting the two conferences. "From the outset, Bishop Copeland's message was one of reconciliation, one of harmony, one of peace, and one of goodwill. . . . In the spirit of love, the bishop brought black and white together as brothers and provided the leadership to accomplish what churchmen consider to be one of the most successful mergers in the history of Methodism."

Chief among black colleagues who worked closely with the bishop to bring about union of the two conferences was Dr. Robert Hayes Sr. Hayes had been pastor of the six-hundred-member Trinity United Methodist Church in Houston and a district super-intendent for six years. For two years he served as Bishop Copeland's administrative assistant and was named president of Wiley College in Marshall, Texas, in 1971. [Wiley is one of the denomination's eleven historically black colleges.] Bishop Copeland served as president of the Wiley College Board of Trustees during the five years he was in Houston, giving the school, in Hayes's words, "new life, new challenges, and a valu-able reason for being."

Hooper Haygood was on the staff of the white conference when Copeland came to Houston. He inter-preted the Texas Conference to black congregations in much the same way Hayes interpreted the Gulf Coast Conference to white churches. "We had many difficult issues, such as the inequity between the salaries and pensions in the two conferences," said Haygood. "Bishop Copeland trusted us and gave us a lot of

121

leeway. He led us through the difficulties in a fine way." Haygood retired in 1994 and resides in Houston.

In 1998, Texas Conference leaders marked the thirtieth anniversary of the elimination of the Central Jurisdiction by producing *Milestones of Faith*, a study booklet "celebrating the African American presence in the United Methodist Church." C. Chappell Temple was pastor of First United Methodist Church in Alvin, Texas, and wrote that Hayes did more than any other African American leader of the time to advance the merger. "Bishop Copeland told him to preach in as many white churches as possible and so he did, though in some places his mission was far from understood by all at first."

To fully appreciate the challenges faced by Bishop Copeland, Hayes, Haygood, and others as they sought to unite the two conferences, it is necessary to understand the racism that was deeply imbedded in the region at that time and the tensions that existed.

Temple talked about three young black men who interrupted the 1969 Texas Annual Conference.

> Though memories of the incident vary, the encounter happened just as Bishop McFerrin Stowe was completing a sermon on the power of the Holy Spirit. Stowe had just said that "the Spirit moves where it will," . . . when the three nondelegates walked into the sanctuary, demanding the microphone to air their grievances which, it was later discovered, included the payment of more than $29 million to a black economic development fund. Though many objected, the conference was immediately adjourned, and the three young visitors were escorted to

meet with church leaders, such as Judge Woodrow Seals,
to hear their concerns.

Despite a common history, polity, and denominational connection, Temple said there had been
relatively little contact between the black and white
conferences. The only thing they shared were the same
geographic boundaries. "When it came right down to
it, we just didn't know each other very well," he
quoted a white pastor as saying. In some areas of the
conference racial separation was even more evident.
Temple quoted a black pastor: "In those days in East
Texas the line had been drawn in the sand: blacks and
whites just didn't mix, especially in the churches."

In a prologue to the *Milestones of Faith* booklet,
Jessie Mae Robinson, an African American whose
husband was a leader in the new conference, praised
the diversity that emerged in the conference after
union. Adapting the words of a hymn, she wrote, "Our
focus is not so much to celebrate what separates us and
makes us different, as it is to celebrate what we have in
common. Moments—thirty years—ago, we did not
know our unity, only diversity. Now the Christ in me
greets the Christ in thee in one great family, woven
together in love."

Her husband, Richard H. Robinson, died in 1991
after serving as a pastor, district superintendent, and
conference council staff member. Mrs. Robinson is
widely known in her own right as a musician, worship
leader, and historian.

"The Copelands were endowed with great sensitivity," she said. "They were a team. Bishop Copeland

placed the right person in the right spot because he had studied them. He knew their gifts, graces, and personalities. He was aware of who people were and as they were and why they were. He had keen insight." Like others who knew of the bishop's history in the small Methodist Protestant Church, she said his minority status at the 1939 church union helped him be sensitive to ethnic minority concerns. "He could relate to us and we to him. In a small measure, he was a minority, too."

Jessie Mae Robinson and Catherine reconnected when they served as delegates to the 1980 General and Jurisdictional Conferences, Robinson representing the Texas Conference and Catherine, the Southwest Texas Conference.

Regarding the merger of the two conferences, Houston pastor H. Eugene Cragg said Bishop Copeland was the right man for the task. "He had great vision and loved people. His courage and devotion to the church was unmatched. It showed through in the merger. He was fair with both conferences. His personality and his character, ability, and spiritual power enabled us to do this merger without any problems." Cragg retired in 1998 after serving twenty-six years as pastor of the eight-thousand-member Memorial Drive United Methodist Church in Houston.

Cragg also praised the leadership of Dr. Hayes. "He was a great preacher and had the respect of everyone. He probably spoke in more pulpits than any other preacher in the conference. He and Bishop Copeland carried the ball regarding merger and did it very effectively."

In Houston, as in Nebraska, Bishop Copeland's leadership style was collegial. Haygood was on the staff when the bishop arrived and was responsible for evangelism, mission, and social concerns, all issues in which the new bishop had strong interest. "Bishop Copeland was very dependent on and trusting of his staff," he said. "We had our responsibilities, and we were expected to do them, but he was very much behind what we were trying to do."

After serving on the conference staff, Haygood was appointed by Bishop Copeland as pastor of West University United Methodist Church in Houston. "Bishop Copeland was the kind of leader who, if he wasn't preaching somewhere, was out listening. I remember he and Catherine visiting our congregation on several occasions."

It was common practice for a pastor from one annual conference to be appointed to one of the larger churches in another annual conferences. According to the Rev. Charles Williams, who retired in Houston in 1994, Bishop Copeland made every effort possible to appoint pastors within the bounds of the conference. The bishop never practiced cronyism with clergy under his appointment, Williams said. "Bishop Copeland may have had some friends who were closer to him than others, but when it came to his leadership responsibilities, he did not play favorites." Williams was appointed by Bishop Copeland as senior pastor of St. Paul's United Methodist Church in Houston in 1970.

Williams was acquainted with the Copeland family long before he knew Kenneth personally.

Bishop Copeland's father was my family's pastor in the early years, and my uncle Lloyd Williams, who died in 1970, was a Methodist Protestant preacher. The two were close friends. Bishop Copeland was very astute in his leadership style, a real bridge builder. He was down-to-earth and had great sensitivity to people. He and Catherine were a team overflowing with compassion. Every concern that came to them, even when it wasn't appropriate, was dealt with sensitively, because they understood that it was always important to the person who brought it. In that sense, both of them shared in the pastoral concerns of the episcopacy with great attentiveness to the needs of both clergy and lay people in the conference.

Serving in Houston, home of the Johnson Space Center, gave Bishop Copeland a close-up and personal relationship with the nation's space program, particularly the Apollo program, designed to land humans on the moon and bring them safely back to earth.

The space age was the topic of an address Bishop Copeland gave at the bicentennial celebration of American Methodism in Baltimore in April 1966. He said individuals continue to feel a great sense of emptiness and loneliness despite scientific and technological advances.

"The space age should have brought us together, but for many it has further enlarged the gulf that separates us," he said. The haunting question of humanity is still the same, he declared: "What must I do to be saved?"

Space Center officials invited Bishop and Mrs. Copeland to witness the launching of two space flights in Florida. Bishop Copeland went alone to one launching because Mrs. Copeland had a previous commitment. She later traveled to Florida by herself to witness a launch. "I was seated with a group of people within sight of the launch and felt the ground shake beneath me," she said.

Astronaut Donn Eisele gave the Copelands a small souvenir flag he took with him on *Apollo 7*, the first manned Apollo space flight. From October 11 to 22, 1968, Eisele, Walter M. "Wally" Shirra Jr., and R. Walter Cunningham circled the earth for 163 orbits, checking spacecraft performance, photographing the earth, and transmitting television pictures.

Astronaut Thomas Stafford gave the Copelands a small Christian flag and Bible he'd carried with him on *Apollo 10* in May 1969. On that mission, the astronauts orbited the moon thirty-one times in a rehearsal for the lunar landing. John W. Young and Eugene A. Cernan joined Stafford on that flight.

Astronaut Neil Armstrong became the first man to walk on the moon on July 20, 1969, a few months after the Copelands moved to Houston. During a second lunar landing later that year, astronaut Alan Bean, a United Methodist, became the fourth man to walk on the moon. Bishop Copeland presented him with a "Churchman of the Year" award at the 1970 annual conference session and honored him as the first United Methodist on the moon. The Copelands hosted a dinner for Bean during the 1972 General Conference in Atlanta and gave him a Bible that had been signed by most of the United Methodist bishops. In a letter of appreciation, Bean wrote, "The Bible is magnificent . . . It is in a prominent place in my study . . . It not only looks pretty, but the material they make the cover out of even smells good."

Bishop Copeland continued to serve the larger church through missions, education, evangelism, and family life. In the last years of his ministry, he served on the General Board of Discipleship, where he gave special attention to evangelistic concerns. He was always an evangelist who believed that the prime function of the church is to make disciples in response to the Great Commission.

During the 1960s and 1970s, a distrust of large institutions emerged in the church as well as the larger society. Caucuses were created to influence the denomination, particularly the General Conference, which meets every four years and is the only body that can speak officially for the entire church.

Ethnic minority caucuses worked for racial justice and equitable representation; liberal groups, such as the Methodist Federation for Social Action, spoke out strongly against the Vietnam war and poverty; conservative groups, such as the Forum for Scriptural Christianity, sought to have more explicit Biblical material included in church school curriculum.

Bishop Copeland, always a reconciler, was distressed by the growing chasm between liberals and conservatives. He often spoke of the need to combine practice and theology, the social and personal aspects of the Gospel.

Racial tensions were especially high two years after the 1968 uniting conference in Dallas. A special session of the General Conference was held in St. Louis. The assembly was marked by protests and demonstrations calling for assurances that the former Central Jurisdiction members and churches would be treated equitably by the majority in the church. The church was also being challenged to address problems of racism and poverty in the larger society. At one point in the business sessions, protestors joined hands and encircled the delegates, a confrontational style that was new in the church and disturbing to some. Individuals who spoke up during the Sunday morning worship services at a downtown United Methodist Church were arrested and jailed.

Black members pushed for guarantees, assurances, and help in overcoming centuries of racial prejudice and injustice. Some white members resisted. The Fund for Reconciliation, created by the 1968 General Conference, drew fire from some white members who objected to grants being made to assertive black organizations such as the newly organized Black Methodists for Church Renewal.

In an interview with *The Texas Methodist* editor Spurgeon M. Dunnam III shortly before the conference, Bishop Copeland expressed reservations about groups in the church pressing for self determination. Asked if he believed the time was coming when a pastor could be appointed without regard for his race, he replied, "As a bishop in the church, I would certainly hope that the appointment of ministers can be based positively on their ability to fill a certain need in a certain set of circumstances at a certain time." Asked if he would consider sending a black pastor to a predominately white congregation or a white pastor to a predominately black church, he responded: "Yes, I would, in prayerful consultation with the church involved."

Bishop Copeland expressed hope that the general conference would give leadership to the church in the area of Christian unity. "I do not believe the church can be operated best by disunited pressure groups," he said. "I think it operates best by persuasion."

He said, "If by self-determination you mean that everyone in the church 'does his own thing' without regard for the larger whole; I reject it. If by it you mean that each group makes its own contribution to the church's total witness, then you have what I have called 'group determination.' If the general conference can make a contribution toward this larger goal, I think it will be a beneficial meeting."

Some local churches and members were unhappy with the actions and pronouncements of the General Conference and threatened to withhold their support for World Service, the lifeblood of the church's world-wide ministries. Bishop Copeland hit the issue head-on in an address at a session of the Texas Conference. "We cannot be sure that every decision made by the General Conference, the Jurisdictional Conference, the clergy, or the laity will be the best decision, or even the right decision," he said.

> We can be sure of the leadership of the Holy Spirit, but we cannot be sure that we will always respond to that leadership in the right way. In fact, we can be reasonably sure that some decisions will be wrong decisions.
> Taking into account the human element, we can be reasonably sure that some of the money we send through

our gifts to the church outside the boundaries of our own
individual parishes will be used unwisely.

The same, he added, could be said of expenditures
in a local church. "This is part of our human dilemma.
I cannot assure you that all of your World Service
money has been used wisely."

Bishop Copeland said he had found himself, on
more than one occasion, supporting the minority in
opposing certain budget items. "Although bishops
cannot vote in General Conference, I have found
myself in opposition to some of the legislation and
some of the positions taken by a majority of the voting
members. I have done so with conviction, and I intend
to continue to exercise that same conviction whenever
I feel impelled to do so. I do not consider myself
disloyal to my Church when I do so."

Over the years, the Copelands made official visits
to more than forty countries. Because of his visits to
several African countries in the late 1960s, Bishop
Copeland and the Nebraska Conference had developed a variety of mission linkages with the
Methodists of Southern Rhodesia, which became
Zimbabwe with its independence in 1980. Ralph
Dodge, bishop-in-exile of Rhodesia Methodism, had
toured Nebraska, as had several black Rhodesian
pastors during the 1960s. Congregations in the state
helped several Rhodesian students study at Nebraska

Wesleyan University and the University of Nebraska in Lincoln.

Bishop Copeland's interest in Rhodesia continued when he moved to Houston. During their visit to the country in 1969, the Copelands met Rhodes Chimonyo, a young man with supervisory and administrative responsibility for a large number of church-related schools in the country. Chimonyo had obtained a teaching certificate in 1957, but was hoping for a university education so he could better serve his church.

At the suggestion of Bishop Abel T. Muzorewa, who succeeded Bishop Ralph Dodge as the first black bishop of the area, Bishop Copeland agreed to help the young educator. Churches in the Texas Conference provided scholarship assistance for him and living expenses for him, his wife, and their young son and daughter. He was accepted at Nebraska Wesleyan University and began studies in August 1969. First United Methodist Church in Lincoln provided nurture and support.

Chimonyo completed his undergraduate studies at Wesleyan in 1973 and then moved to the University of Nebraska in Lincoln, where he earned a master of arts degree in English. Years later, in 1994, he was honored by Wesleyan for his "exemplary commitment and service."

"I had my mind set on teaching in high school when we returned home, hence a degree in linguistics would help," he said. "But the church at home had their own agenda for me." When the family returned home in 1974, Chimonyo taught French at the Old Mutare High School. Early the next year he was named conference and field treasurer, a position he held until his retirement in 1997. His office was in the conference headquarters in the capital city of Harare. Since retiring he has served as secretary of the conference board of trustees.

As treasurer, Chimonyo played a key role in the establishment of an all-Africa United Methodist university in Zimbabwe. Authorized by his Zimbabwe Conference, he and a colleague offered a large portion of the Old Mutare Mission Farm as the site for the university, which has produced more than thirteen hundred graduates since its inception in 1992. Africa University prepares teachers, pastors, counselors, agri-culturists, disaster and humanitarian workers, business people, and other professions to work in communities across Africa and around the world.

Chimonyo said:

> Bishop Copeland and his wife were God's blessing to my family. Besides introducing me to the Texas Annual Conference, he also exposed us to the larger United Methodist Church and universities. My visits to Texas—coming from Nebraska every summer to attend annual conference—allowed me to meet and know many friends in the Texas Conference. All this impacted my life tremendously.

Chimonyo described Bishop Copeland as down-to-earth. "He allowed me to be close to his own family by inviting me to visit their home several times," he said. Citing 1 Chronicles 4:10, he quoted Jabez, who called on God to ". . . bless me and enlarge my border . . ."

"In brief," Chimonyo concluded, "my territory has been enlarged all because of Bishop Copeland."

In 1971, the Copelands visited Eastern Europe and India. A few months before his death, the bishop was one of four United Methodist delegates to the British Methodist Conference. Music was a door opener and an icebreaker for him, even on these international trips. Catherine recalled being at the home of missionaries in South America, waiting for a noon meal to be completed. Two young sons of the missionary couple were delightfully surprised when Kenneth sat down at their piano and played some boogie-woogie music.

Because of his proven skills as a presiding officer, Bishop Copeland was among several bishops chosen to guide a business session at the uniting General Conference in Dallas in 1968 and at the first regular General Conference session for the new church in Atlanta in 1972.

When he presided during evening business sessions in April 1968, delegates were considering a controversial recommendation to remove specific prohibitions on the use of alcohol and tobacco from ministerial requirements. The proposal was approved, but not without an accompanying Resolution of Interpretation. The resolution stressed that the changes "do not relax the traditional view concerning the use of tobacco and beverage alcohol by ministers in the United Methodist Church," but ". . . call for higher standards of self-disciplined habit formation in all personal and social relationships." The statement said that the legislation "in no way implies that the use of tobacco is a morally indifferent question," and added that "in the light of the developing evidence against the use of tobacco, the burden of proof would be upon any user to show that his use of it is consistent with the highest ideals of the Christian life."

Even more volatile and historic was the session over which Bishop Copeland presided in 1972, on the last day of the Atlanta conference. Delegates voted to extend the time of the morning session into the noon hour to approve a firm, mandatory date for elimination of racially segregated annual conferences that had been part of the Central Jurisdiction. The 1968 Plan of Union had provided for a transitional period for the merger of black and white conferences. While Bishop Copeland was in the chair, delegates directed the soon-to-meet jurisdictional conferences to determine the number, names, and boundaries of their constituent annual conferences without regard to race. The four racially structured annual conferences and seven annual conferences with which they overlapped were directed to take all steps necessary to consummate merger no later than July 1, 1973.

Racial tensions remained high across the church; efforts to place black members in leadership and decision-making roles were moving forward, slowly but deliberately. Delegates voted to continue the Commission on Religion and Race, originally intended to last only four years, and also created a Commission on the Status and Role of Women to spearhead efforts to empower women. Both commissions continue today. The conference also marked the first time that delegates formally took a position on the issue of homosexuality, a volatile issue with which the church is still struggling.

10

Resurrection

Kenneth Copeland died unexpectedly at the age of sixty-one. He was in his fifth year as bishop of the Houston Area.

Following a meeting of the World Methodist Council Executive Committee in Mexico City in the summer of 1973, he and Catherine joined friends for a short vacation in Acapulco. They arrived on August 5, and he began to experience health problems which a local doctor attributed to climate conditions.

The next morning, Bishop Copeland had not improved, so they returned home. Friends took them directly from the Houston airport to Methodist Hospital. On August 7, doctors came from the intensive care unit and gave regular reports to Catherine in the waiting room. The first two reports were encouraging, but the third was not. The doctor brought the dreaded news that he had died.

Bishop Copeland's last hours were spent in a hospital known around the world as a premier facility for heart patients. Among its surgeons at the time was Dr. Michael DeBakey, an internationally recognized and respected physician and surgeon who had successfully implanted the first artificial heart in 1966. Bishop Copeland, like his predecessor Bishop Paul E. Martin, had served on the hospital's board of directors during his years in Houston and was personally acquainted with Dr. DeBakey. "He was a brilliant man, but very approachable," Catherine said. "On several occasions, Kenneth watched this master surgeon in action." DeBakey was contacted when the bishop was admitted to the hospital and he would have performed surgery if it had been recommended, Catherine said.

Bishop Copeland was thought to be in good health and had never been diagnosed with heart disease. His most difficult health problem was migraine headaches. Not long before his death, he went to a clinic seeking relief. Specialists recommended a less rigorous approach to his work. Catherine said he made a list of things he would do to safeguard his health, including a less demanding schedule.

"A Service of Praise and Thanksgiving to God in Memory of Kenneth W. Copeland" was held on August 9, 1973, at eleven o'clock in the morning at First United Methodist Church in Houston. Pastor Charles Allen opened the service with the reading of Scripture.

Bishop Paul V. Galloway, who would be called out of retirement to finish Bishop Copeland's term in Houston, gave personal comments. The sermon was given by retired Bishop W. Angie Smith, who died a few months later.

"Few people were ever more thorough in study and in writing and delivery nor more ready in spirit and in prayer," Galloway said of Bishop Copeland. "These were personal characteristics as well as qualities. He lived the redemptive and reconciling ministry. . . . His ministry was to unite people one with another, bringing all together related to God."

Smith said he and his wife, Bess, considered Kenneth and Catherine as their own children. He described Kenneth as an ambassador of Christ and a natural preacher. While the ability to preach can be cultivated, Smith asserted that a natural preacher is born. Bishop Copeland, he said, possessed the "vocabulary, personality, and the ability to stand before a group of people with an understanding of their heartaches, sorrows, joys, successes, and failures, and yet deliver a message that would put wings under their feet and cause them to walk out of the house of God feeling that, 'I am a child of God.'"

Bishop W. McFerrin Stowe gave the benediction: "Lord, we have come to the garden. Once again, we have found the stone rolled away."

A memorial service was also held on August 9, at the Perkins Chapel at Southern Methodist University. The sermon was given by Claus Rohlfs, director of field education and courses of study at the seminary. "It is the nature of Bishop Copeland to be able to inspire persons to grow in grace and the knowledge of the love of God and in that knowledge to love themselves and to be freed up from those hang-ups that so easily destroy us," he said.

An editorial in the August 9 edition of the *Houston Chronicle* pointed to Bishop Copeland's reputation as a "strong and forceful believer in the mission of the church, in freedom of the pulpit and pew and in brotherhood," and described him as a "democratic, approachable" man.

The Texas Conference was in a rapidly growing area of the country, but was not immune to the loss of membership spreading across the denomination in the United States. When Bishop Copeland went to Houston, the combined membership of the two conferences was 252,000. At the time of his death, membership had declined to 244,303. However, the conference soon rebounded. Today it has more than 291,000 members and includes some of the largest congregations in the denomination.

Asbury Lenox had been appointed superintendent of the Houston North District by Bishop Copeland. He said the bishop provided the groundwork and inspiration for the growth that eventually took place in the Texas Conference after his death. "When you plant the seed, it takes time for the harvest. That's exactly what happened in our conference."

Despite Bishop Copeland's limited time in the conference, Lenox said he made a profound impact. "He was such an evangelist. He led a two-day session for pastors on the Holy Spirit and another two-day session on evangelism. He gave specific tips on evangelism for the small, suburban, and downtown churches and stressed that we could not be achievers without the Holy Spirit."

Lenox, who was provost of the conference when he retired in 1996, said both Bishop and Mrs. Copeland had a strong influence on young individuals aspiring to become Methodist preachers. "They endeared themselves to people of all socioeconomic strata and had a great, great ministry among us. They talked about growing disciples and helped create leaders who were sensitive to developing disciples and growth in the church."

Eugene Cragg remembered getting the news of Bishop Copeland's death.

> I was stunned. My first thought was, *How can we afford to lose someone of his character, ability and spiritual power?* He was a special guy. He brought gifts, graces, a clear vision, and a sense of direction to the Houston Area. It was precisely what we needed at the time. He had a great gift of contagious enthusiasm. If you were around him you couldn't be pessimistic very long, because he led you to believe you could do anything.

Like others who were asked to reflect on Bishop Copeland's life and ministry, Cragg pointed to Catherine. "I always thought his and Catherine's love for each other nourished his ministry and gave him added strength to do the job. She is a very special person. They made a great contribution to the life and ministry of the whole church."

Kenneth died relatively young, but he was able to see his grandchildren and experience the joy of their early lives. Patti and Bill Ard had three children: Mary Catherine, named for her grandmother; Kenneth Clay, named for his grandfather; and Amy Suzanne. Sue and

Preston Dial had two children: Debra Lynn and Robert Scott. Despite his heavy schedule as bishop in Nebraska and Houston, he was never too busy to answer a telephone call from grandchildren.

While the Copeland name is stamped in the memory of many who knew him, it remains visible today in at least two locations in the Texas Conference: the Copeland Center at Lakeview Methodist Conference Center near Palestine, Texas; and the Copeland Center at the Chapelwood United Methodist Church in Houston.

The Lakeview Conference Center is located 11 miles south of Palestine and 165 miles from Houston. The center began in 1947, when the Texas Conference accepted a gift of 453 acres of land from citizens of Anderson County. The first summer of camping occurred in 1949; the institution was chartered by the state in 1953.

Bishop Copeland stayed at Lakeview often and spoke at numerous events, including retreats for pastors and laypersons. His cabinet also met often at the center. As the popularity of Lakeview grew, the need arose for a facility that could accommodate large groups of a thousand or more people. At the time, the only place for large groups was an open-air tabernacle that was uncomfortable in the hottest days of summer and not usable during the winter.

One of the groups pushing for a new multi-purpose building was United Methodist Women, which often had more than a thousand people on the campus at a time. The women pledged $10,000 to jumpstart construction of the new facility. As leaders moved ahead with building plans and construction, they learned of the death of Bishop Copeland and decided to name the new facility to honor him.

The new center, now the centerpiece of the campus, was consecrated at a special service on April 23, 1974, and was attended by more than a thousand people. Total cost of the initial building, including furnishings, was $156,000. Today, more than twenty-five thousand individuals participate in activities at Lakeview each year. The estimated value of the thirteen-hundred-acre campus is more than $7.5 million.

Construction on the Copeland Center at Chapelwood United Methodist Church began before Bishop Copeland's death and was dedicated in his memory in 1974. The large facility includes a gymnasium, fellowship hall, youth center, and classrooms.

The Travis Park congregation paid off its indebtedness fifteen years after the devastating fire and only a few weeks after Kenneth's death. The church celebrated with a service on November 3, 1973. The Copeland family honored Kenneth with altar flowers, and Catherine led the congregation in the Modern Affirmation of Faith. The bishop at the time was O. Eugene Slater, who had been elected with Copeland in 1960. The program noted that Catherine and the family had shared Kenneth's "unselfish and inexhaustible love and knew Christ was the habit of his life."

Kelly Williams, pastor at Chapelwood for thirty-six years before his retirement in 1994, said his congregation had a love affair with Bishop and Mrs. Copeland.

"I asked him to preach once, and the congregation enjoyed him so much they wanted him to return. He then preached a revival for us. He loved to preach and was a happy man when he was in our pulpit. It was hallelujah time when he was there."

Williams said the congregation, which had nearly five thousand members when he retired, developed a strong affection for Bishop Copeland, not just because he was the bishop but because of his effectiveness as a preacher and the way he related to people.

"When he preached, he would turn and interact with the choir members. They loved him for it and supported him with their music. My men also really went for him. He was a man's man."

Williams helped organize a group of about eighty men in the church who met occasionally for dinner with the bishop and provided financial support for special projects. "You couldn't think of Bishop Copeland without thinking of Catherine," he said. "They always came together, and we loved her and gave her support following his death."

Carroll Fancher, then pastor of First Methodist Church in Bryan, Texas, recalled that the bishop preached a series of services there three years before his death. "In my exuberance in presenting Mrs. Copeland to the congregation, I said, 'This lady could have made a bishop out of anybody.' The bishop enjoyed that and never let me forget it. In fact, when he called me about moving he began the conversation with, 'This is the man that Catherine Copeland made a bishop.'"

Fancher wrote another introduction for Catherine that he planned to use at the next opportunity. Because of the bishop's death, he was not able to use it, but he did share it with his congregation in the August 16, 1973, issue of the *First Methodist Visitor* newsletter:

> When you meet this lovely lady and come to realize that her beauty is enhanced by her ability, you realize that she could have made a bishop out of any Methodist preacher.
>
> When you come to know this man and bask in the glow of his warm heart and observe the dedication and the native ability, you realize that any woman could have ridden into an episcopal residence on his coattail.
>
> Then, a third fact comes to mind. That fact is that there is an all-wise God. In his wisdom, he brought together these two outstanding persons so that they could not overshadow any other mate.

Bishop W. Kenneth Goodson of the Richmond Area (Virginia), paid tribute to Catherine following Bishop Copeland's death: "She added priceless qualities to Kenneth's life and ministry and to salute him is indeed to salute her." Goodson referred to Fancher's earlier comment about Catherine being a woman who could make a bishop out of any man, and added, "It was easier when the man was Kenneth Copeland."

Following her husband's death, Catherine remained in Houston for four weeks before moving to San Antonio. She had been asked to join the staff of Southwest Texas Methodist Hospital there as director of volunteer services.

"I had worked all my life, but never eight-hour days for money," she said. She initially declined the offer, but agreed six weeks later when the administrator urged her to try the job for six months. She mustered her characteristic chin-up attitude and declared, "I will try to do it!" The six-month trial turned into thirteen years. She later served in a public relations capacity, speaking on behalf of the hospital throughout the region, and was named assistant administrator of patient relations. Catherine retired in 1988 and lives in San Antonio.

In an October 1979 interview with a reporter from the *San Antonio Express-News*, Catherine spoke of the adjustment after the bishop's death. "Life is like an expressway," she said. "You suddenly find you're in a lane marked, 'This lane must turn.' You can't turn back. It's too late to switch lanes. You have to follow a new route to reach your destination."

Catherine continued to serve the church on several levels, and was honored in 1976 with an honorary doctor of humanities degree from Wiley College in Marshall, Texas. In addition to service in her local church, she was a delegate from the Southwest Texas Annual Conference to the 1980 General Conference in Indianapolis, and the South Central Jurisdictional Conferences in Little Rock in 1980, and in Lubbock in 1984.

Because of Bishop Copeland's passion for evangelism and preaching and her love for the church, Catherine has been a faithful supporter of the United Methodist Foundation for Evangelism, which was organized in 1949 by lay evangelist Harry Denman. She served as trustee beginning in 1981, was elected vice president in

1984, and has been honored as one of only three life-time founder members. The foundation is an affiliate of the General Board of Discipleship, but receives no money from the general church. Since 1980 it has channeled more than $15 million in voluntary contributions to a wide variety of programs promoting evangelism within the United Methodist Church. Offices for the foundation are located at Lake Junaluska, North Carolina.

In a tribute to Bishop Copeland published in the 1974 *Texas Conference Journal*, J. Kenneth Shamblin, then pastor of the St. Luke's United Methodist Church in Houston, quoted poet Edwin Markham [*Lincoln, the Man of the People*], saying:

> *"And when he fell in whirlwind, he went down*
> *As when a lordly cedar, green with boughs,*
> *Goes down with a great shout upon the hills,*
> *And leaves a lonesome place against the sky."*

There is no escaping the fact that the death of this great Christian leader leaves a lonesome place against the sky in our hearts. He will be missed in the life of the family that he loved. He will be missed in the life of the Church that he served. He will be missed by countless friends whose lives were blessed by the touch of his life upon theirs. But as one thinks of his own life, our hearts are also filled with as great gratitude. We recall two other lines by the same great poet.

> *"Here was a man to hold against the world,*
> *A man to match the mountains and the sea."*

> God in his majesty and power can make mountains and seas, but he also can make a man to match them. He did this in the life and concerns of Bishop Copeland. He gave himself to the Christian ministry at an early age and the great concerns of the Church captured his heart.

Shamblin was elected a bishop at the next jurisdictional conference in 1976, but much like Bishop Copeland, died in active service in October 1983 with less than a year left in his second four-year term as leader of the Louisiana Area.

Bishop Goodson paid tribute to Bishop Copeland at the Council of Bishops meeting following his death.

> He is still very much alive. His appointment has changed, and as sorely as he is missed here, we would not call him back. His life, which like his voice in song was lifted in such harmony and beauty, is now a part of so much great plan and purpose of God in those regions celestial that we will glory in his attainment and be more strongly committed to the end that our lives will again be united—endlessly.

Often, family members and friends know little of what their deceased loved ones understood and truly believed about life after death. That certainly was not the case with Bishop Copeland. He had preached hundreds of funerals, comforted the bereaved, and spoken and written often about eternal life and the promise of victory over death.

In a letter to a member of his family, written years earlier, he declared, "The whole triumph of the Christian message is in the resurrection of Jesus from the dead. Our message is not simple immortality alone, though this is certain. Our message is resurrection through Jesus Christ our Lord." If someone told the bishop they had *lost* a loved one, he was known to assure them, "As long as you know where they are, they aren't lost."

Some of his most penetrating thoughts and convictions about death and eternal life were included in a sermon he gave for the memorial service at the 1968 uniting General Conference in Dallas:

> Apart from the Christian faith, death is a symbol of man's lost hope, and an indication that the sun has set never to rise again. However, our blessed Lord, in his resurrection, makes clear the dimension of eternal life and brings us past the question: "O death, where is your victory," and to the twin affirmations: "Death is swallowed up in victory," and "Thanks be to God who gives us the victory through our Lord Jesus Christ."

Bishop Copeland also spoke of the investment of faith made by one generation for the next. "Our link with the past is something more than sentimentality," he said. "Because of their sacrifices we can serve. Because of their faith we can fulfill. Because they have established roots we can produce fruits. We are inseparably linked with them—not imprisoned by them. There is a continuity in history moving through every change. The patterns may be discarded—the principles never."

Another time he preached a sermon titled "Living Hope Through the Resurrection," based on 1 Peter 1:3–5 (RSV):

> Blessed be the God and Father of our Lord Jesus Christ! By his great mercy we have been born anew to a living hope through the resurrection of Jesus Christ from the dead, and to an inheritance which is imperishable, undefiled, and unfading, kept in heaven for you, who by God's power are guarded through faith for a salvation ready to be revealed in the last time.
>
> It is unthinkable that human life could be created to exist only a few brief years. It is unthinkable that the hopes and dreams and aspirations of mankind, generated through a few brief years while he is in touch with eternal reality, should be blasted by an act we call death. It is incredible to even surmise for one moment that man has no chance of life beyond the grave.

Other faiths believe in various types and forms of existence beyond the earthly life, Bishop Copeland observed:

> . . . the Christian faith puts substance and reality to this belief in life eternal. It is more than immortality. Immortality means living on, but the Christian belief is more than just living on. Obviously there are some forms of life in this world that would not be worth living on . . . The Christian has another word besides the word immortality, and that word is resurrection.
>
> Resurrection means new life, eternal life, it means quality more than just quantity. It is something infinitely

more than adding an eternity of years to one's life. It means adding an eternity of life beyond one's physical years. Jesus made it quite clear in his prayer in the upper room when he said to the Father: "And this is life eternal, that they know thee the only true God in Jesus Christ whom thou hast sent." In other words, eternal life is to know God! If we know God in the limits of this earthly existence, then resurrection means that beyond the limits of this life, beyond the death of the body, beyond that which is material and transitory is the full life of the spirit which we know as the resurrected life.

That is what we believe in when we stand beside a new grave in which lies the body of a dear one who loved God and served Christ during his earthly sojourn. This is what the minister means when he quotes the words of Jesus at the funeral service: "I am the resurrection and the life; he who believes in me, though he die, yet shall he live, and whoever lives and believes in me shall never die" (John 11:25–26 RSV).

This scriptural reference, he said, is made real while living within the limits of the earthly body.

It is the living companionship of the living Lord who is Lord of life and Lord of death and who lives evermore within the limits of this earthly life as he companions with us and still within the greater context of the life beyond this one . . . He walks with us through this earthly life, up to the very door of death and through it and beyond it! Let nothing shake our faith in this divine companionship of Christ! This is the greatest assurance we could possibly have.

One of the greatest promises ever uttered by our blessed Lord was his promise: "And because I live, you too shall live." He promised his disciples that he was going away to prepare a place for them, that he would come back and receive them unto himself, that where he is there they might be also. And he extends that promise to every human being who will accept him in faith and companion with him in trust day by day . . . Because he lives, we too shall live.

Heaven is wherever Jesus Christ is, Bishop Copeland said. "When you surrender some Christian loved one in death, please be assured that that loved one is with Jesus. The sorrow is on our side, not on the side of the departed loved one with Christ. That departed loved one is now in a fuller life of the spirit where no sorrow, or death, or crying can ever come!"

Faith in the resurrected Christ and in the resurrection will sustain individuals in this life and give them courage to meet death when it comes, he continued. "Death for the Christian is but an open door into the wider ranges of the life eternal." He suggested that individuals make a list of close friends or family members who have died. "I believe that they are conscious of your life here and now and that their love reaches through all of the barriers that seem to divide us in our limited way from them in their unlimited way. You will think about them, thank God for the lives they lived, but especially make sure that you have released them to the greater love of God."

Consistent with Bishop Copeland's counsel to thank God for the lives of loved ones who have died, officials at Lon Morris College released a written doxology of appreciation in the days following his death. The bishop had served as trustee of the two-year United Methodist-related college located in Jacksonville, Texas.

The letter from the college's trustees, president, administrators, and faculty was an expression of concern and sympathy for the family. More than that, it was a tribute:

> Bishop Kenneth W. Copeland lives with us today in that great and noble fellowship, the Community of Saints. He walks with us through the familiar and friendly halls of memory. He speaks with us through remembered and written words dressed for eternity.
>
> Bishop Copeland was a pastor, always sensing with deep feeling and compassion the personal needs of those committed to his care.
>
> Bishop Copeland was a preacher, proclaiming the Word of God with the prophet's scorn of tyranny; and the love of God which is mighty to save.
>
> Bishop Copeland was an author, faithfully committing to print words that speak to the present and future.
>
> Bishop Copeland was an administrator, committed to the creation and maintenance of those structures which serve to the glory of God and tell his message of salvation in the world.
>
> Bishop Copeland was an educator, applying himself as student and scholar to the search for truth; yielding himself as a teacher of the Gospel; and, by the authority vested in him, strengthening and encouraging those institutions to which are committed the responsibilities of imparting knowledge and truth.
>
> Bishop Copeland was a servant of God and a statesman of the church. In these roles he was both

reconciler and bridge builder. As reconciler he brought together those who had been divided; as bridge builder he made it possible for those who had lived separately to cross and walk together.

In closing, the Lon Morris officials praised the bishop:

. . . who by his life has done a beautiful thing for God; who lived among us as one who showed the goodness of the Lord in the land of living; and who blessed us all with memories that will make our lives more meaningful.

Sermons

Proclaiming the Word

Kenneth Copeland's skill and effectiveness as a preacher helped make him the man he was. Thousands of people across the nation and around the world heard him preach. Some representative sermons are included here with the conviction that they can be instructive and inspiring, even today.

It is important to note that the sermons reflect the language of his day. The use of gender-inclusive pronouns for men and women in liturgy, music, and worship was not a major issue in the Church and society at the time.

The following sermons are inadequate, not because of content or quantity but because they cannot possibly convey the power of Bishop Copeland's spoken word. The impact of his message was not determined solely by *what* he said but *how* he said it.

The bishop rarely used a manuscript when he preached, preferring an outline written on one sheet of paper, folded once. Hundreds of these outlines are among his papers in the archives of the South Central Jurisdiction at Bridwell Library at Perkins School of Theology, Southern Methodist University. Manuscripts exist for sermons he gave on special occasions in the local church, or at civic group meetings and large national events. Several of these are shared here.

With practice that began as a child, Kenneth Copeland could preach a sermon on any text at the drop of a hat and with no notes. Even when he no longer was pastor of a local church, he welcomed opportunities to preach to groups of any size.

His sermons brought hundreds into the Christian family and prompted many to go into full-time Christian service. His sermons gave hope to those in despair and guidance to those who were lost; they enabled ordinary people to accomplish extraordinary things.

His heart as a pastor connected with the hearts of his listeners. He felt what they felt. They sensed in his presentation a man of passion called and inspired of God.

The Gracious Calling of the Lord

*This sermon was given by Bishop Copeland at the
Seventh Quadrennial Assembly of the Woman's Society of
Christian Service at Portland, Oregon, on May 15, 1966.*

The words of John Greenleaf Whittier combine with the music of Frederick C. Maker to bring us one of our most beloved hymns: "Dear Lord and Father of Mankind." The second stanza suggests: "In simple trust like theirs who heard, beside the Syrian Sea, the gracious calling of the Lord, let us, like them, without a word, rise up and follow thee."

For man in every generation, the call to follow Christ comes with amazing freshness. The author of the Fourth Gospel tells of the Lord's post-resurrection appearance to the disciples and his conversation with Peter. "Do you love me?" three times he asked. And three times Peter replied, "You know I love you." And each time he commissioned him to feed the lambs, tend the sheep, and feed the sheep. Then he forecast the manner in which Peter would die, and in which he would glorify God. Then he said, "Follow me." Of course he had issued this call to Peter three and one-half years ago. But again he issues it with eternal as well as contemporary implications.

I sincerely believe the great demand of this generation is the Christian demand to follow Christ! The great discovery of this generation will be the discovery of the lordship of Christ! The great decision of this generation will be the decision to follow Christ wherever that takes us! The demand is already with us. The discovery and the decision are ours to make, aided by his Holy Spirit. And make them, we must, if our world is to know either sanity or salvation!

Reflecting on the fact that some are leaving our churches today, John J. Vincent, the English minister who wrote the book, *Christ and Methodism: Towards a New Christianity for a New Age*, [New York: Abingdon 1965] says:

> We have filled the churches with half-Christians for one hundred years with the offer of cheap grace and the present exodus has happened not because we have asked too much, but because our easy demands have seemed utterly incompatible with the hard demands of life. People have left us from sheer boredom. We now need to begin to fill the churches with those who will hear the word, "Follow me!"

The greatest opportunity the Church faces today is the opportunity to discover what it means to follow Christ, and do it with absolute abandon! This will involve a rediscovery of Christ, who he is and what he is. The New Testament records his own testimony that he is the Way, the Truth and the Life. When either the individual Christian or the Church has been in trouble it has been when the true vision of Christ has faded for the moment, the personal presence of Christ has been lost within the tired and confused soul of man, and the clear-cut command of Christ has been forgotten, even temporarily.

Similarly, the days of the Church's greatest glory and of the individual Christian's triumphant victories have been the days when the face of Christ was most clearly seen, the voice of Christ most clearly heard, the way of Christ most clearly perceived, and the command of Christ most perfectly obeyed. We have been told we must "make Christ relevant," but we cannot forget that the relevance of Christ depends on the reality of Christ. The relevance of Christ is not something we make, but a great truth we recognize and to which we respond in faith and commitment.

The Holy Spirit is more eager to renew the Church than the Church is to be renewed, but renewal depends on recognition, and response and revelation. God has revealed himself in Jesus the Christ. He builds the Church on the great truth revealed in Peter's confession, "You are the Christ, the Son of the Living God." He declared, "Flesh and blood have not revealed it unto you, but my Father who is in heaven."

The renewal of the Church will come in precisely the same way: a rediscovery of who and what Christ is, an understanding of what his will and his way are for man, and a supreme commitment to him as Savior and as Lord.

His Great Commission places upon the Church the responsibility of "making disciples of all nations," and making disciples involves belief in Jesus as Savior and following him as Lord. The implication and involvement are staggering!

To begin with, it is most important that we understand the call is from Christ. It is Christ who calls! It is Christ to whom we give answer! It is Christ we follow in discipleship! This is infinitely more than following a great cause, even though exceedingly worthy it may be. It is more than commitment to a high ideal, even though it represents the highest possible in man's aspirations. It is the Christ who calls! It is he who said, "I am the Way," and who repeatedly called to high and low, to rich and poor, "Follow me." And it was by heaven's authority that he called to follow him.

This means Jesus Christ is Lord! He has a right to call! Whether we accept his lordship or reject it does not alter the fact he is Lord. Our accepting him or rejecting him will make all the difference in our lives, but it will do absolutely nothing to change the fact of his lordship. He is Lord of life and death, of heaven and earth. Best of all, he is the living Lord! He is at work in his world, both in the Church and outside the Church. The Christian witness does not "take Christ" anywhere. He is already everywhere. God revealed himself in Jesus the Christ. He is still revealing himself in the Living Christ at work in his world. The author of the Prologue to the Fourth Gospel reminds us, "He came unto his own things, but his own people would not receive him." His own world, his own things! "The earth is the Lord's and the fullness thereof, the world and they that dwell therein."

I am not quite sure what our sociologists mean when they speak of "secular city," or what some of our theologians mean when they speak of "religion-less Christianity." But of one thing I am sure: this is my Father's world—and that means the city as well as the country—whether we call it secular or sacred. The Christian hymn suggests, "Let earth receive her King. Let every heart prepare him room, and heaven and nature sing . . ." Well, earth did receive her King and heaven and nature are still singing but every heart has not prepared him room. And it is to these hearts, and to ours, he still calls, "follow me."

The call is personal, the caller is personal, the response is personal. It is the call of a person to persons, the response of persons to a person. It has its social implications, to be sure, but the call is from a person, the only person who has the right to ask it of persons, "follow me." No other leader of religions asks this, nor can he. Christianity centers in a person in whom the living God reveals himself and in whom we behold his glory, full of grace and truth. The call comes from Christ. It may be heard in Alabama or Angola, in Kentucky or Korea, in Tulsa or Taiwan, in Portland or Peking—and it may be heard through circumstances that seem strangely remote from a Christian atmosphere, but it comes as his call. And the answer must be given to him.

Our response to him, then, moves into a meaningful experience, and experience makes way for witnessing. After all, experience is all we have to which we can witness. We express only what we know to be true, and we know truth only as we have it in human experience. When the Christian witness is able to say to the world, "I have seen the Lord!" then and only then do we have a story to tell to the nations. And until we are able to say, "I have seen the Lord," we have no story to tell.

It has been reported that the artist friends of William Holman Hunt tried to dissuade him from attempting a painting of Christ. "You can paint only what you see," they told him, reflecting their own school of artistry. "You will waste your time trying to do the impossible." Hunt replied, "But I am going to see him. I will work by his side in the carpenter's shop. I will walk with him over the hills of Galilee. I will go with him among the poor, the blind, the lame and the lepers. I will go to Gethsemane with Him. I will travel with him to Calvary and climb to the cross with him until I see him and then I will paint him."

And those who have examined his work, especially *Light of the World*, believe he accomplished his purpose. Sir William Barrett has said, "Whatever the humblest men affirm from their own experience is worth listening to, but what even the cleverest men, in their own ignorance deny, is never worth a moment's attention."

We are being told we should listen to the world, the un-Christian world, and even the anti-Christian world. And there is merit in this admonition. I have been doing some of this listening for a long while, and intend to keep on listening. But I think it is high time someone called us to listen more carefully to the Christ! For the world's heartache is really his heartache, and the hungers that seek to destroy mankind are his hungers which only faithful disciples can fulfill in Christian witness and service.

Yes, it is Christ who calls, "Follow me!" It is to Christ our answer, negative or positive, must be given. He calls. We answer him, we follow him. And at every step in the road some soul is blessed when we truly follow Christ.

The call of Christ to follow him involves an eternal sense of direction. When he calls, the heart of faith might well ask, "Where are you going?" Of course faith does not wait to know all of the details before responding in a meaningful commitment. This would be bargaining with God, and this cannot be true Christian discipleship. But faith, because it is faith and because it is committed, asks for instructions: "Where are you going?"

He once asked two of his disciples, "What do you seek?" They asked in return, "Where are you staying?" Then he replied, "Come and see." And today we ask, "Where are you staying?" "Where are you going?" And he suggests, "Come and see!"

Legend has it that soon after the crucifixion of Jesus, Peter attempted to flee from Jerusalem, only to be met by a vision, and to stammer, "*Quo vadis, Dominie?*" ("Lord, whither goest thou?") And Jesus replied, "Yonder to the city, to be crucified in thy stead." And so we ask today, in a nuclear world, "*Quo vadis, Dominie?*" And the answer comes in a thousand ways, "To the uttermost part of the earth bearing a cross for mankind everywhere. Follow me!"

Where is he going? While we can never give the full answer any time, or even part of the answer all of the time, we can find in the pages of the sacred Scriptures much that sheds light on the direction he takes and that in which he expects us to follow. For one thing, I am sure he is going where persons are, where their hungers and heartaches, their loneliness and their longings, their hostilities and their hatreds tear them apart. He is going where their needs cry louder than their protests, where their hopes beat on the doors of heaven and refuse to give way to hopelessness. He goes to persons with needs and he goes not empty-handed. He goes to hungry people with food, to lonely people with love, to sick people with healing, to the dead with life, to the sinful with forgiveness, to the feeble with strength, and to the defeated with victory. Where people cry out for freedom he is there. Where the exploited lie crushed he is there with dignity and honor. To follow him, therefore, means to go where he goes, do what he does, serve as he serves, and love as he loves.

Most of all, however, it means he is going in the direction of the Father. And if we follow him, we follow him to the God of us all whose love and redeeming grace are made real in Christ. Often he rose long before daybreak to spend time with the Father in prayer. And before he chose twelve disciples he spent all night in prayer.

What a lesson for us there! No wonder we get into so much trouble trying to elect leaders in our churches! We spend perhaps one minute in a kind of invocation before we put down a long list of nominations for office in the church, and then wonder why we come out with problems. But in every hour we need to seek the face of the Father, and most assuredly we will if we follow Christ.

When his final hours on earth came, the "hour of decision," he was found alone with the Father in the Garden of Gethsemane, praying, "Not my will, but Thine be done." Ah! This is it! This is the way of total giving of self to the Father's ultimate will.

And all of this surely means we follow him to a cross. Here we balk. Here we back away. We don't want a cross. We don't want to pay that price. And yet, we can never be his disciple unless we are willing to "deny self, take up our cross, and follow him." Here alone is the true meaning of life. Here is where self is to be found and life is fulfilled, in bearing our cross for Christ.

In this connection, Dr. R. V. Williamson, of Louisiana State University, says the student on campus suffers from what he calls "the Existential Disease." That is, he is able to ask the questions, but is unable to find the answers to "Who am I?", "What am I here for?" and like questions. But he cannot find the answers. Williamson goes on to point out he believes the answers are found in the Christian faith. "Human beings, not just students, professors, and administrators, but all men find themselves in confrontation with God, and God is most fully revealed in Jesus Christ," he says.

> As long as man compares himself with other men only, the self-realization is hazy, partial, uncertain, and ephemeral. Confrontation with Christ, however, engenders a full self-realization whereby man becomes painfully aware of what he is and gloriously aware of what God meant him to be. He knows he is a sinner, not just in general but in agonizingly specific ways. He also knows he is called to be a saint, not just a pale shadowy figure but a living person destined to grow in the likeness of Christ.

Also, he is going to a resurrection, and "because I live, you shall live also." Thank God!

It has been said today's man is restless because he is rootless. This is another way of saying that we need a sense of purpose in life, a sense of direction for life. Daniel Yankelovich, head of a large independent social science research firm in the United States, has remarked, "In the long run, I fear, we will find the crisis of poverty easier to solve than the crisis of purpose." And the noted psychoanalyst, Erik Erikson, speaks of a kind of process going on in young adults—eighteen to twenty-five—which he calls "identity formation." He speaks of the unrest on our campuses today and says it has made us alert to a facet of identity which he calls "the need for fidelity." He says the young adult—and there are now twenty million of them in the United States—at this stage of his life feels an intense need to be true to something outside of himself. For man does not live by affluence alone!

Of course, not many of us in this audience would be bold enough to identify ourselves with this young adult group. For most of us find ourselves somewhere midway between the Pepsi Generation on the one hand and the Geritol on the other hand. But our need for direction and purpose in life is just as acute, and in some cases more serious. If a man does not know where he is and cannot plot his future, he is lost! And, remember, Jesus came to "seek and to save that which was lost."

If we believe he is the way, that he knows where he is going, that he bids us follow him, then by all that faith means operating in human life we can be assured we will have that sense of purpose and direction and that we will not be tossing about on troublesome seas with neither compass nor rudder.

This leads us to the third implication in his call, and that is service. He calls us to follow him in service for others. If he is to be found where persons and their problems are, he is found there in service, giving and giving and giving. Direction would mean very little if there were no destiny, no service. He came not to be ministered unto but to minister and give his life. He came not to be served but to serve. And whatever his call to us means, we can be sure it means service for others. For in some strange way we may never quite understand in this world, God has chosen to work his works among men through men.

And it is no coincidence, I am sure, that he would describe the Last Judgment in terms that come to grips with life on this earth in which service for others, in his name, becomes the measuring rod for rewards and punishment. "Inasmuch as you did it (or did it not) unto one of the least of these my brethren, you did it (or did it not) unto me," he said. And here we find commendation on the one hand—and to be as sincere and direct—condemnation on the other hand.

[Halford E.] Luccock calls attention to a saying by a very wise man: "If a ship is going to ride anchor till she rots, it doesn't make a straw's difference whether her chart and compass are false or true." Luccock goes on then to suggest: "If a life never cuts its anchor and sets out into the great waters of Christian discipleship, it makes not a straw's difference if it be filled with piety and sound doctrine. The great thing is to do God's will."

Service for others is the one way we can fulfill our discipleship for Christ. Albert Schweitzer took the position that the only way one could really love God is through others. You may disagree with the theological stance he takes here, but you cannot deny the fuller implication of our response to God through service to others. Here we see something more radical than identification. Here we are talking about involvement. Anyone can rather easily identify himself with some great cause or some great issue. It doesn't take as much courage to do this as it does to really become involved in the midst of these great causes, especially when we realize that involvement, Christian involvement, is always with persons. In matters of social injustice and exploitation, Christian involvement is at the point of persons within the problem and not just the problem. And let me point out here I am talking about persons in particular and not humanity in general. And our involvement with persons must be at the point of service to them and with them and not just sympathy for them.

Not enough is being said or being done about the service motive in our society today. Much is being said about the profit motive and the power motive, however. We are being told we must come to grips with the power structure and that we must learn to organize community life that will manipulate these structures to the advantage of the exploited and the undernourished. There is some merit in this, to be sure. But what is lacking in the total picture is the importance for the Church of the service motive. In fact, some of those who are most active in community organizational life hold there is no interest beyond self-interest. These reject as naïve and sentimental the idea that any community will ever voluntarily move according to the service motive.

But can there ever be any hope for mankind apart from service for others? With the proliferation of nuclear weapons capable of destroying mankind in a matter of hours, with a growing belief that man acts only in terms of self-interests, with an increasing emphasis on organizing hate to combat hate, what hope can there be? The hope lies in the Christian affirmation that the basin and the towel are companions of the cross and the empty tomb, and that the only way to world peace is through redemptive love and reconciliation expressed in terms of Christian service to mankind. The Christian's choice is the choice of involvement, or the sadness of the silent sidelines.

Of course the Church must steal away for worship and refreshment of soul and mind. But, like Jesus, the Church must come back from its Mountain of Transfiguration to stand level with the crowd where boys lie sick because weak and faithless disciples do not know how to cast out the demons. Here, on the level with mankind, we stand face-to-face with human need and here we must highly resolve to become servants for Christ's sake. This means involvement with man in his illiteracy, in his hunger, in his disease, in his fears, in his failures, in his hopelessness, in his sin, in his death!

When the New Testament calls upon us to "feed our enemies," it isn't talking about some kind of spiritual food the nature of which we have little or no knowledge. It is talking about Nebraska wheat, corn, and beef! A cup of cold water means a cup of cold water. Visits to prison mean real prisons. Ministry to sick people means real sick people. A wise man once said, "The question of bread for myself is a material question, but the question of bread for my neighbor, for everybody, is a spiritual and religious question." [Nicholas Berdyaev, in *Religion That Is Eternal*, G. Ray Jordan]. Surely it is more than a wise maxim to believe Jesus Christ is saying, "He who feeds his neighbor feeds three: himself, his hungry neighbor, and me."

And finally, let us see this call to follow Christ as a call to commitment! It must be commitment to Christ, to his will and his way, to his purpose and power, to his love and his life, and to his service for others. Someone has suggested a better word here is surrender, and perhaps it is. For real commitment means the surrender of sin and self, of what we are and what we have, to be witnesses to and servants of the living Christ. Here we need to come to the place where we can say to Christ, "Wherever it is, Jerusalem or Galilee, however it is, smooth or rough, whenever it is, in winter or in summer, however it is, I will go, dear Lord. I will go to the uttermost part of the earth, to the world across the street from me or the world across the continent from me. Through every wall that divides the human race from each other and from thee, I will go. For I have the assurance thou wilt go with me, even unto the end of the earth." Nothing short of this total commitment will do!

O Jesus, I have promised to serve Thee to the end;
Be Thou forever near me, my Master and my Friend;
I shall not fear the battle if Thou art by my side,
Nor wander from the pathway if Thou wilt be my guide.

O Jesus, Thou hast promised to all who follow Thee
That where Thou art in glory there shall thy servant be;
And Jesus, I have promised to serve thee to the end;
O give me grace to follow, my Master and my Friend.
Amen.

The Glory of the Ministry
This sermon was preached in 1967.

This year, 1967, is the thirty-sixth anniversary of my ordination as a Methodist minister. Born and reared in a Methodist minister's home, I was assigned my own pastorate at the age of twenty years. I have been challenged by two ministerial generations, the generation of my father as well as my own. I first knew the ministry before a minimum salary or Social Security or any promise of a pension as an added enticement. My concept of the ministry as the hardest and the highest calling of man still stands. I also believe it is the happiest. I freely use the word glory with respect to the ministry, because I think it belongs here.

Of course, there is much in the ministry that is not glorious; certainly there is much that is neither glamorous nor glittering. There is nothing glorious about a cluttered desk or a cluttered mind. There is nothing glorious about the endless, irritating interruptions, the subtle backward pulls which struggle against he forward drives, the distractions that demand our time and rob us of opportunities to improve our minds or enrich our spirits, or the thorns in the flesh that always pain and sometimes poison, and the desperation that cries out: "My God, my God, why?"

Perhaps the most unglamorous aspect of the ministry is the frightening recognition that the earthen vessel which houses the heavenly treasure is so very earthen. The desperate struggle in our minds between the man our people think we are and the man we know we are and the man we know we should become is a frightening struggle. But just before the fatality of futility strikes its death blow, we recognize the glorious fact that this earthen vessel houses a heavenly treasure. Simple modesty would forbid our believing there is anything glorious about the earthen vessel, but honesty demands that we recognize the glory of the heavenly treasure and the glory of the privilege which is ours in housing it.

Can it be that the glory of the ministry, or the glory *in* ministry, lies in the fact that we are sent, sent by Christ as his witnesses in a world he created and to people he loves and for whom he gave his life? If we believe that we have this ministry by the mercy of God and that we are sent by Christ with a frightening responsibility, then surely there is glory in the ministry.

The record in John 20:19–24 gives the setting for this affirmation:

> On the evening of that day, the first day of the week, the doors being shut where the disciples were, for fear of the Jews, Jesus came and stood among them and said to them, "Peace be with you." When he had said this, he showed them his hands and his side. Then the disciples were glad when they saw the Lord. Jesus said to them again, "Peace be with you. As the Father has sent me, even so I send you." And when he had said this, he breathed on them, and said to them, "Receive the Holy Spirit. If you forgive the sins of any, they are forgiven; if you retain the sins of any, they are retained." (RSV).

As the Father sent the Son into the world, even so the Son sends us into the world. Is it unbecoming to ask, "How did the Father send the Son into the world?" I think not. While no one of us would presume to know what was in the heart of the Father when he sent the Son into the world, except as the Holy Spirit reveals it to us, yet some things seem clear enough for us to make the relationship between his commission and ours.

In the first place, it seems certain that the Father sent the Son into the world with a message to proclaim and a mission to perform. In like manner, Christ sends us into the world. The message is the glad tidings of God's redeeming love in Jesus Christ for all people in all circumstances at all times in all of the world. It was first enunciated by the angels on that first Christmas night: "Behold, I bring you good news of a great joy which will come to all the people; for to you is born this day in the City of David a savior, who is Christ the Lord."

The message is the message of redemption! The message is his; the proclamation must be ours. The Christian ministry must know the difference between the compulsion of having to say something on one hand and the impulsion of having something to say on the other hand! Our blessed Lord knew quite well where he stood with respect to the proclamation of the Gospel when he announced in the synagogue: "The Spirit of the Lord is upon me, because he has anointed me to preach good news to the poor. He has sent me to proclaim release to the captives and recovering of sight to the blind, to set at liberty those who are oppressed, to proclaim the acceptable year of the Lord." He made it quite clear that he was sent to proclaim God's mercy for man's misery, God's grace for man's guilt.

It is the Gospel we proclaim! We sometimes seek new words to express ageless truths, though we always come back to the fact that it is "God's good news" which we proclaim. We have cheapened the word "gospel" by using it as an adjective to describe some form of religious practice which we usually do not like. We have set an informal and sometimes carelessly arranged Sunday night service over against a more liturgical and orderly Sunday morning service and called the Sunday evening service a "Gospel Service."

We have expressed our disdain for some of the simple songs with simple theology and simple tunes by calling them "gospel songs." May God help us to cease the misuse of a great word. If "What a Friend We Have in Jesus" is a gospel song, pray tell me what kind of a song is, "A Mighty Fortress is Our God?" The Gospel deals first of all with the nature of God who "so loved the world that he gave his only begotten Son, that whosoever believeth in him should not perish, but have everlasting life." The Gospel speaks of a great God, not a limited God.

A theological student once wrote a paper on "The Nature of God," only to discover when it was returned to him by his professor that it had been marked with a C+. He complained to one of his fellow students and said, "I don't see how I am going to preach with only a C+ God." The terrifying answer, of course, is that we cannot!

The Gospel is both real and relevant. It is real if it is biblically based, Christ-centered, and historically verified. It is real if it seeks more to "experience God" than to "explain God." The reality of science is discovered through research and experiment, while the reality of religion comes through revelation and experience. The fruits of the faith are impossible without the roots of the faith.

The Gospel is relevant when it is allowed to speak to contemporary man. We do not make the Gospel relevant; it is relevant when we discover it is real. Reality precedes relevance; relevance is assured if we give reality a chance to work. The changeless Word of God must be communicated in the changing language of man. We must remember that we do not witness to an 1867 world. That world is no more. Neither do we witness to a 2067 world. That world does not yet exist, except in our imagination. We witness to a 1967 world with its racial struggle, its revolutions and rebellions, its Vietnam and South Africa, its "new morality" which some of us believe is neither new nor moral, its standardless society, its hopelessness, and its hunger. We present the ageless Christ to the changing world. Christ is the Word of God whom we present in the words of men.

This is God's good news, and the world is waiting to hear it. In his introduction to Helmut Thielicke's, *The Trouble With the Church: A Call for Renewal* [Harper & Row, 1965], John W. Doberstein has reminded us that "people today are not tired of preaching, they are tired of our preaching." Whenever we find, even in this day, a vital, living congregation, we find at its center vital preaching. The man who cannot preach and will not devote himself to it with the best that is in him is not likely to be any more effective, credible, and convincing, so far as the Gospel is concerned, in a discussion group, a cell group, a buzz group, as a conductor of ceremonies, or as an organizer and manipulator of God's human beings. The Gospel is the message through which the power of God can revolutionize life. God help us to believe it; God help us to proclaim it.

The message is the message of redemption. The mission is the mission of reconciliation. It is quite clear that God has committed unto us this mission, and we must understand that this is a mandate to reconcile man to God. In its initial sense, reconciliation is a one-way street. Man has alienated himself from God, not God from man. Man has rebelled against God, not God against man. God loves the world; the world does not love God. The minister finds himself unrelentingly in the role of the reconciler, attempting by God's grace and through the power of the Holy Spirit to reconcile man to God. "God was in Christ reconciling the world unto Himself, and he has committed unto us the ministry of reconciliation." The preacher, the pastor, the counselor, the evangelist, the person who is made a minister by the grace of God, becomes the reconciler.

The reconciler does not compromise standards or violate principles in order to be a reconciler. On the contrary, if he does violate the eternal principles he ceases to be a reconciler. The minister is the reconciler between man and God and also between man and his fellow man. In this second relationship, reconciliation still in its original sense is a one-way street. The first task of the reconciler, between man and men, is to reconcile each man to God, for when any two persons are close enough to touch the feet of the Christ, they are close enough to touch each other. However, the role of the reconciler is cast in its contemporary sense between man and men. This requires that we know the difference between the sinner and his sins, and our response of love for the sinner and our hatred for his sin. Our blessed Lord was able to look past adultery to the hungry heart of the adulterer, past the act of sin to the soul of the sinner. Reconciliation furthermore involves both identification and involvement, identification with man in redemptive love and involvement with man in his needs, his heartache, and his hunger.

Reconciliation is a costly experience, not without its blood, sweat, and tears. Paul Scherer has portrayed this expensive way of sharing redemptive love when he described it as, "Putting your hand out to help people and jerking it back with a hot, stabbing sting of a nail in its palm." And this is what it is all about! In reconciliation we stand between a man's rebellion against God on the one hand and God's love for rebellious man on the other hand, and this is a dangerous position to occupy. Standing between man's hostility to his fellow man and the recurring hostility of his fellow man to him can be a devastating experience, but this is precisely where the Gospel places us. Reconciliation demands that we help man see himself as he really is and to see God's love as it really is. The reconciler must listen carefully to man's cry, "O that my eyes were opened," and also to God's pleading in Christ, "Come unto me, all ye who labor and are heavy laden, and I will give you rest."

Who is sufficient for this hour? None of us in his own strength is sufficient! It is at this point that the companionship of Jesus, "Lo, I am with you always, even unto the end of the world," comes to have meaning. In this stance, Paul could say, "I can do all things through Christ who strengthens me." Yes, he has committed unto us the ministry of reconciliation, and the only limits that can possibly be set to this ministry are the limits that we set by our prejudice and our pride.

Our blessed Lord was sent into the world with a message and a mission. He believed his message; he was true to his mission. Charles Haddon Spurgeon once said of Luther: "Nobody doubted that he believed what he spoke. He spoke with thunder, for there was lightning in his faith. The man preached all over, for his entire nature believed. He was the incarnation of faith; his heart was running over at his lips." May God give to the ministry today the force of a vital faith to proclaim the message and to perform the mission.

In the second place, it seems evident that the Father sent the Son into the world with a passion and a power. When Jesus looked on the multitudes, either as individuals or en masse, he looked upon them with compassion. Whether as individuals or en masse, they were always persons and he saw them as persons. Demons trembled before him and begged him to send them away from him, but men possessed with demons knew the full force of his love and his cleansing power. Sin was always his enemy, and with the last drop of his blood he fought it and conquered, but the sinner knew that "God so loved the world that he gave his only begotten Son, that whosoever believeth in him should not perish, but have everlasting life."

Brethren, we must love men to Jesus. Great hearts gripped by the great love of God are always the foundations on which great preachers and great pastors are built. We must cultivate our affections. No man can ever be a good minister of Jesus Christ unless he loves people and loves them immensely and redemptively. George Buttrick once referred to the "veritable pain of love," for he knew not only its reality but its cost. People know whether you love them or not. They know whether our ministries are professional or redemptive, whether they are purely formal or actually forceful.

It takes a special kind of caring to fulfill the nature of redemptive love. Here you plead with a man for his own life, not yours. Here his response is measured in terms of his salvation, not yours. This kind of sacrifice is measured not in terms of what you give up but what you give out, not so much in what you are willing to die for as in what you are willing to live for. This kind of love is something more than "a feeling for someone." It is rooted first of all in God's love for man and issues forth to man as we share it with man.

Our blessed Lord sends us not only with a passion but also with a power to communicate this redemptive love to others. Without this power we could not do it, and without our consent God's power cannot do it. The key word here is the word of our blessed Lord immediately prior to his ascension: "You will receive power when the Holy Spirit has come upon you, and you will be witnesses unto me . . ." This is it! The power is not ours; it is the power of the Holy Spirit— God with us.

None of us has this power within him as a natural, human endowment. Each of us knows what it means to come to the end of a busy day with only half the recognizable tasks done, feeling like all strength and energy have gone out of us, wondering how we could ever pick up tomorrow and attempt to help people carry their loads. But somewhere in the still of the night, just before the blessed anesthesia of sleep answers the agonizing hurts of the day, a still, small voice comes to us across the centuries with ever-increasing assurance: "All power is given unto me both in heaven and in earth . . . Lo, I am with you always, even unto the end of the world."

This is the power we can trust. Gripped by this power, we are no longer faced with the equally deterministic alternatives of "suicide or surrender." When we are filled with the power of the Holy Spirit, we do not have to decide between the alternatives of being "red or dead." The Lord is the Savior of men who triumphed over death, over hell, and over the grave to bring life and immortality to light through the Gospel. All power is given unto him in heaven and on earth, and he imparts that power to those who follow him in faith. "You will receive power" is both a promise and a provision and through our faith it becomes fulfilled.

Finally, with all my heart I believe the Father sent the Son into the world with a commission and a commitment. The order was from God. It bore the print of his own finger. It was delivered to the Son firsthand, and it comes to us in the same manner. Of course the Church has a claim on our time and talent. Of course the areas we serve, the parishes to which we minister, have claims on our loyalty and our love. Of course we are answerable to these institutions under whose leadership we work, but our commission is ultimately and finally from God through Jesus Christ our Lord. When I have any temptation to bypass my responsibility to the Church, to the area I serve, or to the parish to which I was appointed pastor, there comes a touch on the shoulder and a voice in the ear and to the heart which says, "As the Father has sent me, even so send I you . . . Go therefore into all the world and make disciples of all nations." I dare not turn from that voice. If there is any heart left within me, I simply cannot!

The commission is a command, and the command is to "make disciples." It is not an elective; it is not one among many delightful alternatives. Of course we have our freedom of choice, and this freedom makes possible our denial of all he asks us to do, and some of us do rebel in this way. But the commission remains a command. It is God's command! And in the face of a command there are only two alternatives: obedience or disobedience. And I must make my own choice between these alternatives.

The commission is his to give, and he gives it. The commitment is ours and it is up to us to make it. Commitment becomes first of all a response to God's prevenient grace in Christ, to God's divine call to us, to God's divine command. "Whom shall I send, and who will go for us?" is still God's divine announcement to the world. "Here am I, Lord, send me." This remains man's response and responsibility.

This is where the sermon concludes and the service begins. No one can make a commitment for another. No minister can make it for another minister, nor for his people. Ministers are made on earth. They are made by God's divine call, to be sure, but they are not made until they respond in commitment for themselves.

This commitment will be made by different people in different ways. Some, like Saul of Tarsus, will make the commitment prone on their faces with the light of God's convicting power blinding them. Others, like Timothy, will grow up with this commitment as an inseparable part of their lives. But somewhere along the road the commitment must be verbalized: "Here am I, Lord. Send me."

Many times our pride and selfishness get in the way, and we have to cry out to God again and again for the help we need to make sure we mean it when we say, "Here am I, Lord. Send me." But God gives grace for every need, and reminds us his strength is made perfect in every weakness. The commitment is still ours to make, and as ministers we must make it again and again. The commitment is to one Lord, one faith, one way, one world, one people. I share with you the conviction that this is the hardest thing we have to do, but at the same time it is the most rewarding. There is glory in the ministry, the glory of God in the face of Jesus Christ.

Many of us find Badger Clark's poem, "The Job," expressing the prayer that we feel over and over again, the prayer of simple honesty and ultimate commitment:

THE JOB
by Badger Clark

But, God, it won't come right! It won't come right!
I've worked it over till my brain is numb.
The first flash came so bright,
Then more ideas after it—flash flash!—I thought it some
New constellation men would wonder at.
Perhaps it's just a firework—flash! fizz! spat!
Then darker darkness and scorched pasteboard and
    sour smoke.

But, God, the thought was great,
The scheme, the dream—why, till the first charm broke
The thing just built itself while I, elate,
Laughed and admired it. Then it stuck,
Half done, the lesser half, worse luck!
You see, it's dead as yet, a frame, a body—and the heart,
The soul, the fiery vital part
To give it life, is what I cannot get. I've tried—
You know it—tried to catch live fire
And pawed cold ashes. Every spark has died.
It won't come right! I'd drop the thing entire,
Only—I can't! I love my job.

You, who ride the thunder,
Do you know what it is to dream and drudge and throb?
I wonder.
Did it come at you with a rush, your dream, your plan?
Yes, with rapt face and sparkling eyes,
If so, I know how you began.
Swinging the hot globe out between the skies,

BISHOP WITH A PASTOR'S HEART

Marking the new seas with their white beach lines,
Sketching in sun and moon, the lightning and the rains,
Sowing the hills with pines,
Wreathing a rim of purple round the plains.

I know you laughed then, while you caught and wrought
The big, swift rapturous outline of your thought.
And then—
Men.

I see it now.
O God, forgive my pettish row!
I see your job. While ages crawl
Your lips take laboring lines, your eyes a sadder light,
For man, the fire and flower and center of it all—
Man won't come right!
After your patient centuries
Fresh starts, recastings, tired Gethsemanes
And tense Golgothas, he, your central theme,
Is just a jangling echo of your dream.
Grand as the rest may be, he ruins it.

Why don't you quit?
Crumple it all and dream again! But no;
Flaw after flaw, you work it out, revise, refine—
Bondage, brutality, and war, and woe
The sot, the fool, the tyrant and the mob—
Dear God, how you must love your job!
Help me, as I love mine.

The Church Triumphant Now

This sermon was preached
between 1960 and 1968.

When we lay our blessed dead away we reluctantly, but faithfully declare we are surrendering them to "The Church Triumphant," to whose rolls they have been added. This is the Church beyond history, and in this dimension it is rightfully to be called The Church Triumphant. It is in this relationship, I am sure, that Paul declares in his famous resurrection chapter, 1 Corinthians, chapter 15, "Death is swallowed up in victory." It is a final triumph when the final enemy is destroyed, the Scriptures declare that the last enemy to be destroyed is death.

With what joy, therefore, do we think of the Church beyond history as "The Church Triumphant!" We are justified in this confidence when we surrender to God the soul of our departed loved one, assured that since he is absent from the body he is at home with the Lord. Even though our hearts ache at the outward and visible sign of separation, our faith triumphs in the assurance that not only is our dear one at home with the Lord, but in a very real sense is also more spiritually "at home with us" than was possible in the flesh.

Not only as individual believers in Christ, but also as a Church is this ultimate triumph to be realized beyond history. In God's blessed heaven the Church emerges completely triumphant over death, hell, and the grave. Nothing to be said in this message to minimize the significance of this ultimate triumph beyond

185

history. In fact, the ultimate triumph beyond history adds impetus and meaning to the triumph I wish to discuss with you relevant to and in history.

If we agree that the Church beyond history is The Church Triumphant, and I am sure we will agree, must we think of the triumph of the Church only beyond history? Is there no way in which it functions in history triumphantly? The Scriptures would seem to indicate there are areas of triumph for the Church in history. In 2 Corinthians 2:14, Paul declares, "But thanks be to God, who in Christ always leads us in triumph, and through us spreads the fragrance of the knowledge of him everywhere" (RSV).

Paul would have us understand that this triumph in history, as well as beyond history, roots in Christ's triumph both in and beyond history. Surely he had knowledge of the fact that his blessed Lord had declared, "All authority in heaven and on earth has been given to me" (Matt. 28:18 RSV). Surely he must have been reflecting on this when he said to the Colossian church:

> And you, who were dead in trespasses and the uncir-
> cumcision of your flesh, God made alive together with
> him, having forgiven us all our trespasses, having
> canceled the bond which stood against us with its
> demands; this he set aside, nailing it to the cross. He
> disarmed the principalities and powers and made a
> public example of them, triumphing over them in him.
> (Col. 2:13–15 RSV)

And who among us could possibly overlook the affirmation of 1 John 5:4–5 (RSV): "For whatever is born of God overcomes the world; and this is the victory that overcomes the world, our faith. Who is it that overcomes the world but he who believes that Jesus is the Son of God."

If he is the head of the Church, if he has all power in heaven and in earth, if he has promised victory to the faithful followers, if he has made clear the vocation of the Church, if the Church is true to her Lord, cannot we expect the Church therefore, within the still recognizable limits of human nature, to be The Church Triumphant within history? I sincerely believe we can.

How can the Church be the triumphant now? It would seem that the New Testament standard for triumph is clear. First of all, I would suggest the Church can be The Church Triumphant to the extent that it fulfills its role in revelation. The Church does not exist first of all as an institution whose chief responsibility is to teach a new way of life. Of course Christianity teaches a new way of life, but this is the fruit of its faith, not the root. There are those who passionately protest that Christianity is not a theology, but a way of life. Of course, Christianity reveals a way of life, the best way of life known to man or possible to man. However, the role of the Church is not first of all to reveal a new way of life, but first of all to reveal the living Christ who is the fullest possible revelation of God to man.

Let me suggest a revision of this statement: The Church's role in revelation is a permissive one—God is to reveal himself through Christ, and the Church's supreme task is to be the channel for that revelation to be given to the world. In other words, the world must see the living Christ in the church. Now if the world cannot see this revelation in and through the Church, then pray tell me where can it see the revelation?

Paul set the tone for his own preaching when he declared, "we preach Christ crucified." Anyone can preach about Christ, teach about Christ, sing about Christ. In fact, in certain circles it is quite the popular thing to do, talk about Christ. But the supreme task of preaching, teaching, and witnessing from the Christian point of view—and these are the primary responsibilities of the Church—is to reveal the living Christ.

"He that hath seen me hath seen the Father," our blessed Lord assured the doubting disciples as he continues to assure a doubting world. And the Church exists for the prime responsibility of letting this light shine so that others may see and glorify God. In fact, as Luke records in the opening verses of his message to Theophilus, in the book of Acts, Jesus made it clear that the task of the disciples was to be witnesses unto him, in Jerusalem, Judea, Samaria, and unto the uttermost part of the earth. The prime responsibility of the Church, therefore, is to witness not simply to a way of life or the standard of ethics, as valuable as these are and as necessary as they are, but unto Christ in order that the world may see God as revealed in the face of Jesus Christ through the witness of the Church.

Now the most casual among us would admit that we have done many things as a Church which not only did not reveal the spirit and face of our living Christ, but to our shame and embarrassment revealed a spirit in opposition to our living Lord. And in these the Church stands in judgment, judged not by a critical world or even by a godless Communism quite so much as by the living truth itself, by the Christ who said, "I am the way, the truth, and the life."

A word of warning needs here to be said to those critics who look at these lapses in the Church's execution of its God-given responsibility and say, "If that is religion, I don't want it." Most of us would agree we don't want that kind of religion either, but the Church has failed in its responsibility when it has revealed some shoddy brand of religion, some counterfeit, instead of the living Christ himself. To the critic I would say, look not to some counterfeit interpretation of religion for your estimate of the genuine. Look for the face of Jesus Christ, and then and there determine your acceptance or rejection of him.

Much of our exclusiveness would seem to drive Christ from us. Much of our petty jealousies would place him on the periphery and ourselves in the center. Let us as a Church enthrone him as King of Kings and Lord of Lords. Let us as a Church declare him as the living Christ. Let us as a Church allow him to live in us, reveal himself through us to the world.

We are the Christian Church! That which distinguishes us from other religious bodies is not our system of ethics or our standard of morals, even though we believe these standards excel all others. That which distinguishes the Christian Church from other bodies is that at the center of what it preaches and urges its

189

followers to practice is the living Christ. Ours is a faith in a person, not a program. Ours is security rooted in a savior, not a system. Our power is his who promised, "All power is given me in heaven and in earth. Go ye, therefore, into all the world and preach the Gospel to every creature." Our strength is not dependent upon a sort of moral escalator on which we might happen to be clamoring for a position, but on him who said, "Lo, I am with you always even unto the end of the world."

It was on this rock Christ built, and is building the Church. "Thou art the Christ, the Son of the living God," declared Peter, and this declaration has become the cornerstone of our Christian theology. God questions man in Christ, "Who do you say I am?" And man responds in faith, "You are the Christ, the Son of the living God." Now where you have this question and this answer you have the Church. You might have a building and budget, a parson and a program, a choir and a crowd, but you don't have the Church. Where man confronts God's question in Christ and responds with man's answer and faith you have the Church, whether the building is small or large or the membership is to be numbered by thousands or ones.

I confess I am sometimes disturbed when people speak of a given church as "one of our great churches." I do not resist the use of the great in this connection at all. I think there are some great churches. What disturbs me, however, is the fact that usually when the term is used it refers to a church that has a large membership. I had the responsibility of being the pastor of one of those churches for eleven and one-half years, and I was always proud to hear it called a great church. However, I confess to you in utter sincerity that the greatness in that church lay not in its size, but in its service, its theology, and chiefly its insistence on the personal experience with Jesus Christ as Savior and Lord. Any church is a great church which seeks honestly and sincerely to reveal the living Christ to the world.

It is significant that the only affirmation on which the ecumenical movement is to be based and which the participating Christian bodies are expected to be in complete agreement, as witness the standard for fellowship within the councils of churches, is recited in the simple words, "I believe Jesus Christ is God and Savior." This is the final basis for any unity of Christian churches, whatever their size or structure. Perhaps it is not far from the truth to declare it is the only necessary basis for Christian unity around the world.

Let the Church recover its role in revelation, the revelation of God in Christ. God grant that in our worship and our witness, in our labor and our life, and our prayers and our program, in our teaching and our training, the world can see Christ! The Church can be The Church Triumphant in history now, to the extent that it fulfills its role in revelation, even within and through the limits of our human feeble efforts, through the power of his Holy Spirit.

The Methodist ritual for the reception of members would here remind us, "Dearly beloved, the Church is of God." Let Methodists never forget this! To the extent we allow his spirit to breathe the breath of God upon us, to the extent we allow the face of Christ to be seen in ours, to the extent we make real the picture of God in Christ, to that extent the Church can be The Church Triumphant now. And I pray God it may be.

Furthermore, the Church can be The Church Triumphant in history to the extent it fulfills its role in relevance. The Church speaks to today or it doesn't speak at all. Surely it draws on the values and examples of yesterday, and indeed it must if it has any word for today, but its voice must be heard today if there is to be any voice to be heard tomorrow. Surely the values of today will strengthen and serve the generations tomorrow, just as the values of yesterday will serve and strengthen the generation today, but the voice must speak to our years that can hear today, to minds that can understand today, and to hearts that can respond today. We simply cannot afford the luxury of retreating into an old-fashioned yesterday unredeemed. Neither can we afford the risk of projecting our voice into a fantastic tomorrow with its gadget-filled world while today's hunger brings on a quick starvation because spiritual food was being canned for tomorrow's consumption.

No one of us ever opens the pages of the past without thanking God for the voice of the Church which helped in that day to shape the destinies of men and spoke to its world. In spite of many failures—and history does record those also—she saw banners unfurled in many places and in many ways and addressed herself to her task. Luther's reformation and Wesley's revival made their contributions for which succeeding generations will rise up and thank God for all time to come. Surely we will go back frequently and restudy those earth-shaking events, appropriating for our times the lessons which are time-less and eternal. But, we will do it for our time and not for Luther's time or Wesley's.

Liberalism, in any generation, always faces the danger of being tempted to forget the values of the past and history has recorded some incidents of capitulation in this regard. But it is a weak expression of rebellion against such liberalism to keep calling for a return to an old-fashioned religion. We cannot cure illnesses of liberalism, if indeed it has illnesses, by insisting on going back to yesterday for our patterns while all other forms of society insist on going forward. Neither can the failures or weaknesses of conservatism—and we must admit there are weaknesses and failures in conservatism—be cured by throwing out the baby with the bath water. The Church is commissioned to speak to its day. We believe in the communion of saints, past, present, and future. But our message is to today's saints, and more especially to today's sinners.

We need to be reminded this is precisely what Jesus did, he spoke to his day and in language they could understand. Of course he drew on the riches of the past. He unearthed more buried spiritual treasures than any before him, or since, had done. He knew the Holy Scriptures and was able to debate their meaning with the doctors and the lawyers. He spoke with the timeliness which projected the message piercingly into every tomorrow the world will ever know. But he was relevant. He communicated with his day in language and thought forms with which they were familiar. He spoke of birds and flowers, sowers and seed, bread and meat, sickness and health, death and separation, sorrow and joy. He spoke to little children in language they could understand and to aging folk in words they could appropriate. He spoke of catching fish and shipping commerce. He opened the eyes of those who were blind in his day and raised the widow's sons to life again. He knew the meaning of friendships and forgiveness, and reserved his most intimate description of God and his relationship to his people for a picture of home and family life, for God is called our Father and we are his children, brothers and sisters of each other.

What I am really trying to say is this: to be relevant the Church is under obligation to take the timeless word of God and present it in the timely language of men, the unchanging truth of God in the changing expressions of men, the eternal principles of God through the earthly patterns of man.

This relevance must take into account not only worlds and languages, but human needs. It might sound pious to suggest that man's needs have been the same in every generation and every situation, but this just does not tell the whole story. Ours is a world of scientific progress and technological advance, and Christ has a word for that kind of world. Ours is a world greatly shrunken in the last few years and Christ's message covers all of it. Man's fear of extinction might be basic in every generation, but we must understand the fear which grips the hearts of man on the brink of a thermonuclear war which could destroy civilization as we know it cannot be dealt with in the same way man's fear was met as he stood with bow and arrow in his hand defending his home against an invader. Both our danger and our deliverance are all wrapped up with the human race today. The racial tension which grips much of the world today, the international problems which have brought the nations tottering on the brink of war, hunger and starvation in much of the world, are all very real to today's man and the Church cannot afford to fail to speak to these needs.

Jesus Christ is the same yesterday, today, and forever, thank God! But woe to us if we endeavor to reflect him and his power to today's world in the thought patterns of yesterday's world. Woe also to us if we imprison this timeless Christ in the prisons of yesterday's world, calling all the while to man to go "back to Christ," or "back to religious revival," while Christ's voice calls us to go forward to him, to catch up with him, to move forward in faith.

Great care should be taken in this matter of relevance. In our search for the right word, the right phrase, the right illustration which will communicate to our day, we cannot afford to lose sight of the word which is eternal and changeless. Can we say it this way: to be relevant, the Church must go back of the words to discover the word, whether yesterday's words or today's or tomorrow's, but in so doing it is equally obligated when it does discover the way to transmit it in words which are relevant, and it must be applied to needs which are contemporary.

In some cases this will mean a change in words and vocabulary, for some of our vocabulary has greatly changed across the years. In other cases it will mean taking the same words that were used in yesterday's world, or most assuredly in the New Testament world, and being careful to make clear the meaning to today's world in a language that can be understood. I do not call for the overthrow of the use of great theological words. We have done too much of this, much to our sorrow and shame. But what I do call for however is an insistence on the part of the man who preaches the Gospel and teaches it to attempt to throw light on the deeper meaning of these words.

Yes, let the Church be The Church Triumphant today. Let it speak the message of God to the minds of man. Let it preserve the timeless treasures of its spiritual heritage and apply them to the changing frontiers of man's physical, mental, social, emotional, moral, and spiritual world. Let the Church fulfill its role in relevance.

Finally, I would suggest the Church can be The Church Triumphant to the extent it fulfills its role in redemption. Now all of us know that redemption is the world of God in the heart of man and in the life of man and his world. We know God's plan of redemption is designed for man and for society, that it is God's plan and God's provision. We know that man can neither save himself for his society, that it is only "by grace are you saved through faith," by God's grace operating through Jesus Christ in the heart of man. Our fathers in the faith were correct when they sang, "Jesus paid it all, All to him I owe; Sin had left a crimson stain, He washed it white as snow." But neither our theology nor our conscience will allow us to forget the Church has a responsibility under God to carry out the redemptive process in the world in which it has been placed. God so loved the world that he gave his only begotten Son, but the Church must tell this good news to the world. Surely God loves the world, but the Church must make real that love for the world. The Church that fulfills its role in the world does so as a redemptive fellowship. When it is at its best it is a fellowship of the forgiven and the forgiving.

I had placed on the outdoor bulletin board of a church of which I was pastor one time this statement: "This church is a hospital for sinners, not a social club for saints." And indeed it must be if it is The Church Redemptive. When the Church excludes anyone who has need, regardless of his social standing or his estimated human worth, his race or his position, it ceases to be the redemptive fellowship and cannot possibly lay claim to being The Church Triumphant. When it excludes anybody from its redemptive fellowship it has lost its reason for existence.

It might well be said—although we say it with a broken heart and we say it not judgmentally—that we have made our least progress in this area perhaps. It is reflected in our dealings with human beings of every race and color around the world. Could it be that this failure to love redemptively and to let that love be known is reflected in our declining membership and attendance in the church schools, for example? It has been said that enrollment in the children's division, average attendance of the whole church school, and additions to the church on profession of faith will rise or fall at the same time in the same proportions. The Church does not have to shout from the housetop, "I do not care what happens to you," to show that it does not care. Neither does it have to say loudly, "I care for you," to prove that it really does. Its role in redemption is obvious in the day-by-day steps it takes in an effort to reach the heart of man and to show that it cares, and whether or not it fulfills this role is equally obvious.

The Church's chief role in redemption is to be a channel through which Christ's redemptive love can be made real in the mind of men and reach the heart of man in visible expression. The New Testament agape, the overall divine regard for the welfare of man, must be made real to man and I sincerely believe this is the primary task of the Church. In fact, might we go far enough to say the Church has no business in any relationship in which it cannot express itself redemptively.

It is absolutely necessary for The Church Redemptive to face the indisputable fact of the totality of God's love. God's love excludes no one. He loves all men, or he loves no man, as we understand his love to be shown in Christ. God's love never depends on the worthiness or willingness of the subject to receive it. Neither is it turned away by those who refuse to accept it. God does not extend his love under certain circumstances and at certain times to certain people and then withdraw it under other circumstances and at other times from other people. There is absolutely nothing you can do that will stop God loving you! You can reject the benefits of his love and be lost without these benefits. You can refuse to accept his love for yourself. You can deny the existence of his love. You can turn your face from his love. But you cannot stop the outflow of his love. His love is final, absolute, irrevocable, and undiluted.

Now this is the divine love the Church reflects, if it is The Church Triumphant now. Paul Sherrer speaks of this love in this vivid analysis:

> And so this New Testament, to keep you from seeming too large, stands you up, not by the side of immensity—after all, what does that matter—but by the side of love. And you can't see how long it is or how broad; you can't see how high it is or how deep. It goes trailing its gigantic shadow down little lanes in Palestine, and across the threshold of a widow's home. With its hand it touches everything it sees, making no parade, eager to believe the best, never mindful of its own, knowing how to be silent. And when at last it lays out its young arms on a beam of wood, and answers the first stroke of the hammer with a prayer that has been bothering this humanity of ours ever since, "Father, forgive them, for they know not what they do."

Yes, this is the redemptive love which must find its vivid and vital expression through the Church if it is to be victorious in today's world.

Now this is the redemptive love the Church must reflect. First of all, the Church must believe it. It will do little good to attempt to tell about it if the Church does not believe it. Secondly, the Church must give evidence of its creed by its deeds. This calls for more than pious phrases about salvation and life eternal, and I would not in any measure cheapen the significance of these great words. It calls for demonstration in those areas of human need waiting to respond to love as the Stradivarius waits to respond to the touch of the master violinist. In fact, the only way these great words salvation and life eternal can come to have meaning at all is to see them projected through our lives to the lives of others about us.

Thirdly, this redemptive love must become the motive for everything the Church does. As soon as it majors in saving itself, it will lose itself. As soon as it allows its motives for service to arise out of selfish desires, it begins to disintegrate. The Church must somehow make its Lord's affirmation its own: "I came not to be ministered unto, but to minister." Its outreach will be based on love, regardless of who or what the person's thought is or has been. What a difference this will make in our relationship with other races and other nations! What a difference this will make in our ecumenical activities! What a difference this will make in our total program, when redemptive love motivates all that we do as a church!

Yes, the Church can be The Church Triumphant now as it fulfills its role in redemption. The commission of our Lord is built upon it: "Go therefore and make disciples." And from this command there is no honorable discharge. Our own Methodist Board of Education reminds us the goal of all Christian educators is to lead the pupil to accept Christ as Savior and follow Him as Lord in daily life. They assure us, "There is no place where the task of the Christian educator stops and that of the evangelist begins." Furthermore, they affirm, "The church school teaching which is not designed to lead to this commitment is not Christian education." This is our task, and without its fulfillment we cannot be The Church Triumphant.

Redemption is good news. The Church is called upon to declare it and demonstrate it. And as it fulfills its role in revelation, in relevance, and in redemption, the Church can be The Church Triumphant now. Of course triumph that is complete and perfect form and in its fullest sense is the church beyond history. There human frailties give way to divine perfection. When Christ shall have delivered up the kingdom to the Father, the Church becomes truly The Church Triumphant forever and ever. There, "death is swallowed up in victory!" There all the redeemed can sing without limit, "Thanks be unto God who gives us the victory through our Lord Jesus Christ!" And for all this we look hopefully, and to all this we have confidently surrendered our dear ones whom we have loved long since and lost for awhile.

But this hope for the future serves only to make more real the triumph of the Church here and now. If Christ's power is all power in heaven and in earth, then the Church now can share that "all power" of its Lord, its head. The fear that grips the hearts of so many now should give way to a faith in the spirit's triumph in and through the Church. The Church needs again to join in Handel's glad hallelujahs, "Hallelujah, for the Lord God omnipotent reigneth!"

God give us the insight and intellect, the decision and dedication, which will open our minds and hearts to the living Christ, who will this day in and through us make The Church Triumphant now, to his honor and glory and for the salvation of mankind. Amen.

The Voice of God From Above and the Knock at the Door Below

This sermon was delivered at University Park
United Methodist Church in Dallas on August 22, 1971.

The Scripture (Acts 10:1–21, 34–35) lesson tells the story—an exciting story indeed—of a very devout man, judged by all the standards of religion in his day and in our day. The word devout as it refers to Cornelius of Caesarea, is a most appropriate word. He was a religious man. He was in the exercise of his daily prayers on one occasion when God suggested that he send a group of men to Joppa—which was two days' journey in the transportation of that day—and inquire for one named Simon who resides as a guest at this moment in the house of another Simon by the seashore and bring him here that he may import the fuller meaning of the Word of Life to Cornelius. So Cornelius summoned two of his servants and a military orderly, whom the Scripture takes time to point out was himself a religious man, and set them on their journey to Joppa.

On the second day they drew near to Joppa. It was about noontime and Peter, weary and hungry, had gone to the housetop to await the preparation of the meal. While there he had a vision, a vision which was repeated twice more, making three times the vision came. The New English Bible describes it as a vision of "a great sail cloth let down from heaven slung at the four corners" and on it was a whole host of creatures, creatures that fly and walk and swim. And a voice said to Peter, "Rise, kill and eat."

Peter, with his rigid tradition of the division of food into clean and unclean, said, "No, Lord, I have never eaten anything unclean." The voice said, "Don't ever call unclean what I have cleansed." Twice more the vision came.

Then the voice said to Peter, "There are some gentlemen downstairs. They have come for you. I have sent them. Go down and accompany them without fear." Peter went down and met these strangers and invited them in to partake of the hospitality of his host and hostess and spend the night. On the next day they set out for Caesarea where, after he had preached the full Gospel to Cornelius and his household, Cornelius was baptized in the Christian faith.

Now we would do well to ponder the tension of that moment when both sounds were ringing in Peter's ears at one time: the voice of God from above and the knock at the door below. For this, at any moment in history, is the crisis for the Church, standing always as it must between the housetop of inspiration and the door of responsibility, between revelation and response, between the deed of God and the need of man, between the message and the mission, between the Redeemer and those who cry out to be redeemed.

It is my contention that the Church, when it has been at its best in history, or the Church when it is at its best today, or the Church when it will be at its best tomorrow, will always be at the precise point and at the precise time and in the precise spirit in which it attempts to hold this duality of the Gospel in a meaningful tension. When it neglects either one for the other, its effectiveness fades to the degree of that neglect. It isn't a question of compromising for a middle-of-the-road position, politically, economically, sociologically, or otherwise.

This is what I believe to be the stance of the Bible, both the Old and the New Testaments, both the call of God B.C. and the call of God A.D. Always we must place ourselves in that creative tension and hold that delicate balance between the appropriate emphasis of the call of God from above and the knock at the door below. Woe be to the Church when at any time in its history it either closes its heart to the voice of God or closes its ears to the cries of man!

In that creative tension certain facts seem to be increasingly clear. One is this: Always the Church must find itself standing between a rediscovery of the majesty of God on the one hand, the misery of man on the other hand. We need to rediscover what worship is all about. Now I know there are those who write books and who preach sermons or write editorials saying that all of this business of buildings and assemblies and organizations and structure is an idle waste of time; that the Church finds its mission out there where the people are. Therefore, we should sell our buildings, all of our clergymen should earn their living in some secular way and the Church should simply relate to the needs of people out there.

There is enough of truth within it to challenge us; there is enough of error to be damaging and dangerous. None of us is going to doubt the fact that the Church must find its mission out in the world, but what I contend is that the Church has no motivation for mission out in the world except as it comes to rediscover its meaningful experience with God.

It is my contention that the Church is the called-out assembly for worship and is the sent-out assembly for witnesses. It is my contention that we have nothing to witness about except what we have come to understand of God and his care for the needs of humanity around the world. This is not something that some new theology or new philosophy has advocated. This is the stance of the Old Testament. For it was not until Moses, in his fright and in his retreat from his people, had come face-to-face with the voice of God in the burning bush that he was able either to understand or to interpret or to respond to the needs of his people back in Egyptian bondage.

This is the stance of that beautiful and meaningful story in Isaiah who, in the year that King Uzziah died, saw the Lord high and lifted up and his train filled the temple. It was only after Isaiah had seen the Lord that he saw himself as a sinner and felt the cleansing power of God, and then heard the voice of God: "Whom shall I send and who will go for us?" At that point, and only at that point, was Isaiah able to say, "Here am I Lord, send me."

This is the stance of the New Testament, for it was not until three disciples had gone to the Mountain of Transfiguration with Jesus, where the glory of God in the face of Jesus Christ was so amazingly revealed, it was not until this experience, which Peter tried to keep with him always as an experience in retreat from the world, that the disciples were able to go back into the valley where a sick boy was crying to be healed and make some contribution in the name of Christ to the healing of this lad. This is not an argument. It is a fact of life.

And so the Church must rediscover what the majesty of God is all about, and to this rediscovery we dedicate our message and our prayers and our efforts. This is something more than a meaningless piety which seeks to escape the stark and stern realities of the world. This is the search of a hungry soul for the only thing that adds meaning to life, for the only base on which our concern for mankind can possibly rest and out of which it can be motivated.

But if we believe that—and I do—the other side of the coin is equally true. To run into worship as an escape from reality is, at best, a kind of an escapist theology and, at worst, a retreat from responsibility. For the other side of the coin is equally true. I do not believe, for example, that we truly worship unless that worship not only has its roots in God but moves out to produce fruits for the good of mankind.

I have said that I do not believe we can witness until we have had a meaningful experience with God in worship. The reverse is also true. I don't think we can really worship unless in that worship there is the full intent and commitment to move out in response to the call of God to the needs of mankind. While, as James Stewart puts it, "The imperative of God's mission to the world rests solidly on the indicative of the mighty acts of the Incarnation, the cross and the resurrection and that the dynamic for our unaccomplished task is the accomplished deed of God." The same emphasis can move, on the other side. If we come to understand better the accomplished deed of God then we must move to accomplish our unaccomplished task in the service of mankind.

Both the Old and the New Testaments make it revealingly clear that while we must love God with all our heart, soul, mind, and strength, we must also love our neighbor as ourselves. And the New Testament zeros in on this with a bit more incisive language when we read, "He that says he loves God and hates his brother lies."

So here the Church stands. It must always stand between the majesty of God and the misery of man. The Church dare not close its eyes to the fact that there is more human suffering in the world today than there has ever been. You cannot draw a neat, thin line of geography or of politics or of economics and isolate this suffering from our Christly concern. For all around the world, from the ghettos of America to the refugee camps in the Middle East and Pakistan and India and Africa and Europe, around the world are human hearts that cry, human stomachs that hunger, human bodies that die, human spirits that are imprisoned, and humanity by the millions asking, "Is it nothing to you, all you who pass by?"

The tragedy of the story of the man who fell among thieves between Jerusalem and Jericho was not that the priest and the Levite were priest and Levite. The condemnation is not that they were on their way to worship. The condemnation is that they passed him by, and that they failed to associate the majesty of God with the misery of man.

Lines from one of the folk songs popular today reveals this inner tension: "I'm looking for eternity in this world of misery. But what is really wrong with me, I am not free." Let the Church not only rediscover what is meant by the majesty of God in terms of human experience, but also what is meant by the misery of man. And only when this creative balance is maintained can a church fulfill its mission in the world and that for which Jesus Christ died.

There is a second fact that finds its projection in and through this story, and that is the invitation of Christ on the one hand and the command of Christ on the other. It is the same Lord who said, "Come unto me all ye who labor and are heavy laden and I will give you rest" who also said, "Go ye therefore into all the world and make disciples of all mankind." It is no longer a debate between the personal and the social. God save us from those who would swing the pendulum to either extreme. Our stance must be a stance that holds in creative balance Christ's invitation on the one hand and Christ's command on the other. The Gospel is relevant, it is as relevant when it repeats Christ's invitation, "Come unto me all ye who labor and are heavy laden and I will give you rest," as it is when it commands that we go into all the world and make disciples of all nations.

Our living Lord still calls men to come with hungers to be filled, with hopelessness to be changed into hope, with all of the frustrations to be changed into faith, with all that makes life meaningless to be changed into meaning. This is not discoverable simply on the side of poverty or on the side of minorities. Mankind around the world is filled today more extensively perhaps than in any generation with fears that torment and harass and hostility that eats away like a cancer in the inner body of mankind. And the Church must never forget that it is Jesus Christ, the living Lord, who continues to say to all mankind, "Come unto me. Come unto me. Come unto me and find rest."

But it is the same Lord who said, "Go into all of the world." The Church that he has called out of the world for comfort and for rest is the Church he sends out into the world to witness to his divine grace and love. To refuse to come unto him is to deny ourselves of that element of salvation which is as real as it can be. The element of forgiveness and comfort and rest. To refuse his command to go into all of the world is to refuse to fulfill the fuller implications of the Gospel. And so it is this Lord who stands among us today, who calls us today, who continues to send us. The Church is a body sent. The Church in mission is the Church in movement. The Church that does not go is gone. The Church that makes of its pulpit bomb-proof shelter and of its building a simple retreat from life and locks its doors against the cries of humanity is a church no longer, but a museum. And I would plead with all of the passion in my heart, not only that the Church reemphasize the call of Christ to those who suffer inwardly as well as outwardly, but that the Church would remember that the same Lord sends it out where people breath and burn and swear and sweat and die that it might make its witness real in the lives and affairs in the hearts and minds of people. Always, always we stand between the voice of God from above and the knock at the door below.

Finally, let me suggest that this story also would reveal to us that creative tension that we must always hold between creed on the one hand and commitment on the other. I have lived in the generation in which there was the struggle between the so-called personal and social gospel. I grew up in a period of time when that tension was quite real and when the polarization was intense. I recognize on the surface today much of that polarization returning and I regret it significantly and internally. For there can be no contest between creed and commitment. There can be only harmony.

There can be no swinging of the pendulum either to creed exclusively or to commitment exclusively. For when we do this we damage not only that from which we swing in extremity, but we damage that to which we swing in our extremity. Here it is. It is important what you believe. It is important that we have a biblical and a theological rationale for what we do. What reason do we have to go into all of the world? Why should I care that there is likely to be an aggregate of ten million Pakistani refugees in India by Christmas of this year if present hostilities continue? Why should I care that there are a million and a half refugees in the Middle East? Why should I care that South Vietnam has been devastated and more than a million refugees are there? Why should I care for all of the wars and tragedies of the past or the present? Why should I care if more than half of the world's population will go to bed hungry tonight and many will die on the streets of the cities of our world today unnoticed and unloved and uncared for? Why should I care?

Why should I care except for the fact that I believe these are God's children and I believe there is one God and Father of us all and I believe human life is made meaningful in the fact of God's creation and Christ's incarnation. Except for the fact that I believe that these are my brothers and sisters, I did not choose them. I did not make them. Brotherhood is not your creation and mine. It is God's creation. We have one Father. We have one God. We have one Creator. It is he who made us brothers. Whether we act like it or not, we are. And in this biblical stance I stand and on that foundation I make my place and mission in life.

Now it is important that we believe, but it is equally important how, and to what we are committed. If I believe that God is the Father of us all; if I believe that we are brothers and sisters in creation; if I believe that Jesus Christ died for all mankind; then I'm going to have to do something about it. You see, Jesus Christ did not die for principles. He died for persons—red, yellow, black, and white; east, west, south, and north; old, young, aged, rich, poor—all of us. Now if I believe that, then I must make a commitment of my life, my resources, my energy, whatever I have that can be used of God. That commitment is a commitment of myself. If I can't commit myself, the commitment of my dollars or my efforts mean very little. I must commit myself first of all to Jesus Christ, second to humanity.

Bishop Gerald Kennedy said that a friend of his used to say, "I am fond of the human race because my family belongs to it—and part of my wife's family." Well, whether the friend of the bishop recognized it or not, all of his wife's family belongs to the human race, and because we believe that God is the Father of us all, then I must commit myself not only to the Christ who is God incarnate in human flesh, but to the humanity for which he gave his life. I must commit myself to the realization of the mission and the witness of the church to fulfill that purpose for which Christ gave it birth. And in that commitment I stand this morning.

I thank God for the vision of Peter. I thank God that together at the same time he heard the voice of God from above and the knock at the door below. I am grateful for the fact that he responded both to the voice of God and to the knock at the door. That is the response the Church calls its people to make in these days.

There is a prayer of Asa, king of Judah, on the eve of a great battle which expresses the spirit of what I have been trying to say. He prayed, "O Lord, our God, we rest on thee and in thy name we go against this multitude." Now to come to rest in the Most High and then in the strength of that experience to go out against the powers of darkness and the battle for the kingdoms of the Lord. This is essential worship. This is the true missionary church. "Fair is the moon. Clear as the sun and terrible as an army with banners." In that name and spirit we go.

Let us pray: O God, our Father, we thank thee for the Christ who calls us and who commands us. We thank thee for the church that supports us and sustains us. We thank thee most of all for the God and Father who created us and who commission us in his sight. Accept our commitment this morning as being real and meaningful and give us strength for the struggles and light for the way. Through Jesus Christ our Lord. Amen.

God's Moment

This sermon was preached in the chapel of
Oral Roberts University in Tulsa on February 28, 1973,
approximately six months before Bishop Copeland's death.

There are some words in the New Testament from one of the newer translations, [if] you read it in your translation [you'll] notice the difference. I'm reading from the forty-first verse of the nineteenth chapter of St. Luke's Gospel. I am reading it from the New English Bible because of a certain line I'll make obvious a little bit later on. But you notice the differences, you read along silently when I pick up verse forty-one.

Before doing it, you will remember that this follows his triumphant, or this is a part of his triumphant entry into Jerusalem where they had put their olive branches in the way and shouted Hosanna and some of the religious leaders had said, "Make your disciples keep quiet." And Jesus had said, "If they keep quiet, the stones will cry out." And immediately following that verse then we pick up verse 41. "When he came in sight of the city"— now this is at the Mount of Olives. I stood on that Mount of Olives not long ago and overlooked Jerusalem. The Mount of Olives looked down an embankment to the Garden of Gethsemane and then the valley which in the New Testament is called the Valley of Gahanna and then a little rise and you see the city of Jerusalem.

> When he came in sight of the city, he wept over it, and said, "If only you had known on this great day the way that leads to peace, but no, it is hidden from your sight.

But a time will come upon you when your enemies will set up siege works against you. They will encircle you and hem you in at every point. They will bring you to the ground, you and your children within your walls and not leave you one stone standing on another because you did not recognize God's moment when it came."

Now that's the translation which intrigues me. "You did not recognize God's moment when it came." Other translations use the words, "You didn't know the day of your visitation," but let me use it from this translation: "You did not recognize God's moment when it came."

I suspect the greatest concern I have as a clergyman, churchman, and as a friend of both age and youth is that in today's world, 1973, we will not fail to recognize God's moment when it comes. There are three presuppositions I should like to make without development, and without dialog and then move into development of what I want to say.

The first presupposition is, God's moment is obviously his moment, not just mine and yours; a moment of politics and economy, not simply the moment of the university, the moment of the city, or the moment of the country, the nation, or the race. God's moment is his moment. And we lose ourselves if we don't ground ourselves there first.

The second presupposition is that God's moment is always now, not yesterday, even though there is so much from history that we can learn and there are so many values and so much that can help us in charting our course today. But we don't live in the past. There is a very great and wonderful hymn that I don't want to spoil for you, for I still sing it with great meaning: "Faith of our fathers, living still, in spite of dungeon, fire, and sword." It's a wonderful hymn, but I am waiting for somebody with poetic imagination to write a hymn that says my faith is living, not just the faith of my father, as good as that is, but my faith. So, God's moment is now. It's always now.

The third presupposition is that God's moment, whatever it is, is his gift to you and me. Now put these three presuppositions in your mind for a moment. God's moment is his moment; God's moment is now; God's moment is his gift to us. Now go back to the text as rendered in the New English Bible, "Oh Jerusalem, Jerusalem, and he wept over the city. You did not recognize God's moment when it came." He still weeps over the city. It may be Moscow or Milwaukee, it may be Boston or Bethlehem, but he still weeps over the city, and he is still saying to this generation as he said it to that generation, "Oh, the blindness of so many of us, you don't recognize God's moment when it comes."

Now, what is God's moment? I'd like to try to answer that in three ways:

First of all, God's moment is always a moment of revelation. It is a moment in which God is trying to push through the barriers that humanity has set up between persons and God to reveal himself. Read the Old Testament. Through Moses, through Abraham, through Isaac, through Jacob, through the prophets, through the songs of Israel, and ultimately and perfectly and finally in the incarnation where God

made himself manifest in the human dimensions of
Jesus, God was seeking to reveal himself.

Oh, it isn't difficult to think of God's revealing
himself in those experiences of joy and delight that
capture our imagination and make us smile and lift our
eyes and make us shout and sing for joy. It's easy to say,
"I saw the Lord," on occasions like that, and these are
to be coveted and we seek them and we find them and
we count them numberless though they may be.

It is not difficult to see God revealing himself in the
face of a newborn baby. Those of us who are parents
remember the first baby and how precious and
wonderful it was to hold in your own arms part of your
own life and flesh and blood and bones and personality and yet something distinct, something new and
something in God's own creation.

It isn't difficult for a clergyman to hold a baby in
his arms in any kind of service of dedication, in any
way the churches dedicate their babies to Christ, and
see the face of God.

It isn't difficult to walk through a rose field in east
Texas where they grow them so profusely and to see the
deep reds and the beautiful pinks and the bright yellows
and the mingled colors of the roses and to look into
every rosebud and somehow believe that here God, in all
of his artistic beauty, surpassed anything that man could
ever surpass and say, "God's trying to reveal himself in
his beauty and his creativeness and in the petal of a rose."

Well, one could go on limitlessly, but it's difficult to
turn the coin over. But we have to do it and we will
remember that Isaiah said it was in the year King Uzziah

died, his dear friend, "in the year that King Uzziah died, I saw the Lord."

It's difficult to go into the foxholes in times of battle, it's difficult to go in the hospital for cancer in Houston and hold the hand of a cancer-ridden patient and to be able to come from that experience and say, "I saw the Lord revealing himself."

Now we must keep in mind the fact that God reveals himself in incidences he did not create. For sickness is not the will of God. Health is the will of God. War is not the will of God. Peace is the will of God. But in times of extreme conflict and frustration and fears and hatreds and hostilities and brutality and man's inhumanity to man, in a messy, dirty, bloody world, God's trying to reveal his face in so many ways and so many places under so many different kinds of circumstances. And the person is to be pitied who doesn't recognize God's moment of revelation when it comes.

Now you have your own way and you could add to my list innumerable ways by which you have come face to face with God, in which you recognized the presence of God and that's God's moment and that's where it has to begin. If it doesn't begin there, it doesn't really begin.

All of our concern for humanity as valuable, as loveable, as beautiful as this is, as needful as it is, has little meaning beyond a mature humanism, unless it grows out of first of all an understanding of who God is. Of course he reveals himself supremely in Jesus Christ. That's what the incarnation is all about. In the beginning was the Word, the *logos*, the great fact of life, the central reality of life, that word covers a wide range. In the beginning was the *logos* and the *logos* was with God, the *logos* was God and the *logos* became flesh and dwelt among us. Jesus did not reproduce the Father, Jesus did not reflect the Father, God revealed himself in the human dimensions of Jesus Christ.

God is the initiator, not the flesh or humanity, God takes the first step. My flesh still tingles with excitement when I remember the great oratorios of the choirs at Christmastime, particularly when they sing Handel's *Messiah*, and especially in that tremendous chorus where they reach back into Isaiah and sing, "For unto us a child is born, unto us a son is given. Unto us, and the government will be on his shoulders and his name shall be called Wonderful, Counselor, the Mighty God, the Everlasting Father, the Prince of Peace."

You see, it's always unto us. God started unto us before we could ever begin our journey unto him. God loved us before we knew how to love him. God came all the way to us, every step of the way to us, before we took any steps toward him. That's what the cross is all about. *Oh Jerusalem, Jerusalem, you could have been saved. I wanted to save you, but you didn't recognize God's moment of revelation when it came.*

Let me suggest the second way. I think God's moment is not only a moment of revelation, I'm sure that God's moment is a moment of redemption. I think it is that moment wherever in history it occurs or however it occurs. I am not one of those who seeks to impose upon another the form and pattern by which God reached me.

Paul never did it. His dearest friend was Timothy. Paul had a climactic conversion experience. There's no record in the New Testament of any climactic conversion experience for Timothy. The only reference that's made is made by Paul who said, "I remember the faith that dwelt first in your grandmother and then to come to you and to me."

I'm talking about the fact, not the form, but the *fact* of redemption. Wherever at any given point in time or space or place God confronts a human soul who is willing to be confronted and who is willing to say to God, "I've sinned and come short of the glory of God. Dear God, forgive." In that moment is God's moment of redemption. Oh, the plan was made, the price was paid, the cost was given. Calvary will never be again. It was once and for all. You don't crucify Christ over again. Paul said he died once and for all, and the resurrection followed that, and he arose from the dead once and for all. All of that has been done, but now God's moment of now is the moment of redemption.

Any humanity never stands higher, a person never stands higher, than when he or she bows or kneels or prostrates himself or herself in prayer and says, "God, be merciful to me, a sinner." For in that moment everything about the grace of God moves into that person's heart and life. You see, the majesty of God is not his mystery but his mercy. The Gospel does not center in man's guilt but in God's grace. It is redemption by whatever explanation you give it, which is God's moment. *Oh Jerusalem, I wanted to save you but you didn't recognize God's moment of redemption.*

The third place, let me suggest that God's moment is also a moment of reconciliation, not only reconciliation first of all obviously between man and God, not between God and man. See, God has never rejected us. God has never turned his face from us. God has never hated us. We've turned our face from him. We have refused to love him. So reconciliation between the person and God is always between the person and God. And that's where it begins, but reconciliation is also between person and person. Paul talks about it in that fifth chapter of Second Corinthians where again in this new translation he comes to a kind of *gloria in excelsis* when he says the love of Christ leaves us no choice.

War is not the will of God. Any kind of war is not the will of God. Peace is the will of God, and I'm not talking simply about the cessation of armed hostility. I used to be a pastor. I counseled more in marital situations than in any other, and the greatest warfare and hatred and hostility I've ever seen, I've seen in the eyes of husbands and wives toward each other. I shall never forget the first time I heard a teenage girl say, "I hate my mother."

Now we grew up—in my family, my father is a minister—we grew up where everything was love and we reared our two daughters that way. And everybody kissed everybody else good-night before we went to sleep and no matter when they came in from their dates later on in their growing years, we were still awake and there was still that good-night kiss.

I just didn't know what it meant for a teenage girl to say, "I hate my mother," but it's there. It's there and it's all over the world. It's not only a dividing line between North and South Vietnam, it's not only Checkpoint

Charlie between East and West Berlin, through which I walked a few months ago. It is not only that invisible line between the old city of Jerusalem and the new city where Jews and Arabs (treat) each other with hostility that you just can't even number, account for. But it's sometimes in your own home, or across the street, where the reconciliation needs to be made.

It doesn't mean agreement. It doesn't mean compromise. It doesn't mean somebody being swallowed up by somebody else's idea or ideology, but anytime one hand reaches out to another hand and says, "I love you; God loves you. I don't agree with you but I love you and accept you, my brother, my sister," that's reconciliation and until the world comes to that, we will hasten toward our own suicide. *Oh Jerusalem, you didn't recognize the moment of reconciliation, God's moment, when it came.*

Finally, let me suggest that God's moment is always the moment of my response. And God can come toward me, and he has all the way toward me, but somewhere down the road, somewhere down the line it's necessary for me to make some kind of response to God. Jesus said, "I stand at the door and knock," and the Holy Spirit does stand at the door and knock. But, you see, Jesus is a gentleman. He never breaks down a door and rushes in uninvited. He won't do that. "Behold, I stand at the door and knock. If any will open, I will come in." Where he leads me I will follow. You know, Jesus' invitation was not, think as I think, agree with me, but *follow* me. Now that's an action word. That means he's going somewhere. You talk about taking your stand for something. It's a matter of following Jesus.

SERMONS: PROCLAIMING THE WORD

Where is he going? We have a right to ask that. I don't know every place he's going, but I know some places he's going. I know he's going where sin is and needs to be forgiven. I know he's going where sickness is and needs to be healed. I know he's going where hunger exists and needs to be met. I know he's going where fears are and need to be replaced by faith. I know he's going where persons need him and that's what the ministry is all about and that's God's moment. Any time you and I make one response to the invitation to God, that becomes jointly God's moment and your moment. And your part is up to you.

All of you are much too young to remember, except as you've been told, about the days of the Depression. I lived in those days in 1929, the days of the Depression. The best-seller was Lloyd C. Douglas's book, *The Magnificent Obsession*. Oh, you've heard the story. It's an old one. It was the story of a doctor, a famous surgeon, who had a magnificent obsession of helping other people without their knowing it. He would provide money for scholarships for students like you and they never knew where the money came from. That was his magnificent obsession.

He had a heart condition. He would spend six months working and then six months out at his home on the lake and they had a resuscitator and his wife knew how to use it in case of a heart attack.

One season he was out on this lake in his modest cottage and around on the other side, as the story goes, was a magnificent palatial house in which a wealthy playboy spent his hours and days. And this wealthy playboy, (Bobby Merrick) was out on the lake in his sail-boat and it turned over they finally got into shore and they thought he was drowned and somebody remembered that Dr. Wayne Hudson around on the other side had a resuscitator. So they sped around and got the resuscitator and brought it back and through its efforts revived this wealthy playboy. But while they were doing so, Dr. Hudson had a heart attack and died.

They made a movie out of it in color, one of the first movies in color. The movie left out a scene which the book included. If you remember the book, you remember that the nurse was portrayed in the movie by a redheaded, attractive young woman. Nancy Ashford was the name of the nurse, and she was in the room of this wealthy playboy during his recuperation. The book includes this monologue.

> "You have something very valuable besides money; but you'll never use it." Her tone was judicial, prophetic. "It's in you, all right, but it will never come out. Nobody will ever know that you had it. The money will always be blocking the way . . ." She had taken his hand in hers, maternally. Disengaging his eyes, she stared upward absorbedly, and murmured, as if quite alone, "He'd never do it, of course . . . Couldn't . . . Wouldn't . . . Too much money . . . It would be too hard . . . but God! . . . What a chance!"

I don't know whether you and I will do it or not. It will be costly—God's moment. It may take a long time. It will be very difficult. But, dear God, what a chance. Amen.

Chronology

1912   April 3: Kenneth Wilford Copeland is born, Bexar, Arkansas, to John Wesley and Nancy (Hively) Copeland [married October 1, 1896]. His father is a farmer and supply pastor in the Methodist Episcopal Church South.

1918   Moves with his family to a farm at Midlothian, near Chandler in Lincoln County, Oklahoma.

1924   Makes a public profession of faith at the age of twelve, kneeling at the altar of a brush arbor beside a small country church near Chandler.

1926   Moves with his family to Sparks, Oklahoma.

            Experiences God's call to preach at age fourteen while attending revival services at a church of another denomination in Sparks, Oklahoma.

            Preaches his first sermon during a revival meeting conducted by his father at Warwick, Oklahoma.

            Moves with his family to Wellston, Oklahoma.

1927   Moves with his family to Krebs, Oklahoma.

1928   Moves with his family to Quinton, Oklahoma, where his father and family members transfer their membership from the Methodist Episcopal Church South to the Methodist Protestant Church.

1929   Moves with his family to Wortham, Texas, and then to Corsicana, Texas.

CHRONOLOGY

1930   Graduates from Corsicana High School, enrolls at Westminster College, Tehuacana, Texas.

1931   Ordained as elder in the Methodist Protestant Church and begins serving as his father's associate at the Methodist Protestant Church in Corsicana.

1932   Receives his associate degree from Westminster College and is appointed pastor of the First Methodist Protestant Church in Cooper, Texas. His father is appointed to the church at Slocum, Texas.

1933   October 5: Marries Catherine Andrews in San Angelo, Texas.

1934   September 26: Becomes a father with the birth of Patricia Ann, at their parsonage home in Cooper.

     Attends classes at East Texas Teacher's College, Commerce.

     Appointed as pastor of the Methodist Protestant Church, Dallas, Texas, and attends classes at Southern Methodist University.

1937   September 7: Becomes father to second daughter, Martha Sue, born at Baylor Hospital in Dallas.

1938   Receives BA degree from Southern Methodist University, Dallas.

     Elected as president of the Texas Conference of the Methodist Protestant Church with offices and parsonage in Mexia, Texas.

CHRONOLOGY

1939   Elected as alternate delegate to the conference in Kansas City that unites his Methodist Protestant Church with the Methodist Episcopal Church and the Methodist Episcopal Church South to create the Methodist Church.

1939–40   Receives his first appointment in the new denomination as pastor of a congregation in the outskirts of Wichita Falls, Texas.

1940   Serves as a delegate to first Methodist South Central Jurisdictional Conference in Oklahoma City.

1940–44   Appointed as pastor of First Methodist Church, Haskell, Texas.

1943   Named "Outstanding Citizen of the Year" in Haskell, Texas.

1944   Appointed as pastor of First Methodist Church, Stillwater, Oklahoma.

1947   Takes graduate courses at Garrett Biblical Institute, Evanston, Illinois.

1948   Elected as a clergy delegate from Oklahoma to the Methodist South Central Jurisdictional Conference in El Paso, Texas.

1949   Appointed as pastor of Travis Park Methodist Church, San Antonio, Texas—one of the top ten churches in the denomination.

1951   Receives honorary doctor of divinity degree from Southwestern University, Georgetown, Texas.

CHRONOLOGY

1952   Visits Europe, accompanied by Catherine, Sue, and Patti.

            Serves as a clergy delegate from the Southwest Texas Conference to the Methodist General Conference in San Francisco.

            Serves as a clergy delegate from the Southwest Texas Conference to the Methodist South Central Jurisdictional Conference in Wichita, Kansas.

1952–60   Serves as a member of the Methodist General Board of Evangelism.

1954   Visits Methodist work in several South American countries.

1955   October 25: Faces the tragedy of a fire at Travis Park Methodist Church.

1956   Serves as a clergy delegate from the Southwest Texas Annual Conference to the Methodist General Conference in Minneapolis, Minnesota.

            Serves as a clergy delegate from the Southwest Texas Annual Conference to the Methodist South Central Jurisdictional Conference in New Orleans, Louisiana.

1958   September: Leads his congregation's move back into its rebuilt and remodeled church building.

1960   Serves as a clergy delegate from the Southwest Texas Annual Conference to the Methodist General Conference in Denver, Colorado.

Serves as a clergy delegate from the Southwest Texas Conference to the Methodist South Central Jurisdictional Conference, hosted by Travis Park Methodist Church in San Antonio.

June: Elected a bishop at the South Central Jurisdictional Conference in San Antonio.

June 26: Consecrated as a bishop at the altar of Travis Park Methodist Church.

Assigned to a four-year term as bishop of the Nebraska Area of the Methodist Church.

1960   Receives an honorary doctor of sacred theology degree from Nebraska Wesleyan University, Lincoln.

1960–68   Serves as a member of the Methodist Board of Christian Social Concerns and as chairman of its Division of Peace and World Order.

1960–72   Serves as a member of the Methodist Board of Missions (1960–68) and is president of the World Division of its successor, the United Methodist Board of Missions (1968–72).

1962   October 19–December 2: Visits Methodist work in Southeast Asia, including Singapore, Taiwan, Hong Kong, and Japan.

1964   Returns to the Nebraska Area for a second four-year term.

           Receives an honorary doctor of laws degree from Southern Methodist University, Dallas.

Delivers sermon at the closing worship service for the Fourth National Conference of Methodist Men at Purdue University in Lafayette, Indiana.

1964–68   Serves as member of the Methodist General Committee on Family Life.

1966   Delivers sermon at the Seventh Assembly of the Women's Division of the Methodist Board of Missions, Portland, Oregon.

Serves as fraternal delegate to the Mexico Methodist General Conference in Monterrey, Mexico.

1967   August 14–November 10: Visits Methodist work in Hawaii, Korea, Japan, Okinawa, Hong Kong, the Philippines, India, and Pakistan. Also visits projects of the World Council of Churches in Turkey, Iran, Israel, Greece, and Italy.

April 16: Participates in a dedication ceremony at the Church Center at the United Nations in New York for a sculpture, *Prince of Peace*, given in his honor by the Nebraska Conference Women's Society of Christian Service.

1968   Presides over a business session of the General Conference in Dallas, where the United Methodist Church was created with a union of the Methodist and Evangelical United Brethren churches.

Assigned to a four-year term as bishop of the Houston Area of the United Methodist Church.

CHRONOLOGY

1968–72   Serves as a member of the United Methodist Board of Discipleship.

1969   Presides over the last sessions of two conferences in the Houston Area: the Gulf Coast Conference of the former Central Jurisdiction and the Texas Conference of the South Central Jurisdiction.

          September: Visits African countries, including Rhodesia, South Africa, and Zambia.

1970   June 1: Presides over the union of the Gulf Coast Conference of the former Central Jurisdiction and the Texas Conference of the South Central Jurisdiction, Jones Hall, Houston, Texas.

          Presents Churchman of the Year award to astronaut Alan Bean for his accomplishments as the first United Methodist on the moon.

1971   July 10–23: Attends continuing education sessions in Oxford, England.

          Visits Methodist work in Eastern Europe.

          Visits Methodist work in India.

1972   Serves as a member of the United Methodist Board of Discipleship.

          Presides over a business session of the 1972 General Conference in Atlanta.

          Preaches to an ecumenical gathering of approximately five thousand people in Ocean Grove, New Jersey.

Serves as one of four United Methodist delegates
to the British Methodist Annual Conference,
Newcastle-upon-Tyne, England.

Assigned to a second four-year term as bishop
of the Houston Area of the United Methodist
Church.

1973   June 4–7: Presides over his last Texas Annual
Conference sessions at First United Methodist
Church in Houston.

August 5: Becomes ill in Acapulco, Mexico, after
attending a meeting of the executive committee
of the World Methodist Council in Mexico City.

August 7: Dies of a heart attack at Methodist
Hospital in Houston, Texas.

August 9: Memorialized at a service held at First
United Methodist Church in Houston, Texas.

August 10: Buried at a graveside service at
Mission Burial Park in San Antonio, Texas.

September: Succeeded by retired Bishop Paul V.
Galloway, who completes his 1972–76 term as
leader of the Houston Area.

Bibliography

Agnew, Theodore L., *The South Central Jurisdiction 1939–1972: A Brief History and an Interpretation*, Walter N. Vernon, ed. Oklahoma City, Commission on Archives and History, South Central Jurisdiction, The United Methodist Church, Nashville, Tenn.: Parthenon Press, 1973.

Beeson, M. A. "Dr. Beeson Writes of the Copelands." *Travis Park News*, 4 March 1949.

"Bishop Copeland Was Able Leader" editorial. *Tyler Morning Telegraph*, 9 Aug. 1973.

"Bishop Kenneth W. Copeland" editorial. *Houston Chronicle*, 9 Aug. 1973.

Copeland, Kennard Bill. *Reminisces and Recollections: Sixty Years Together—Bill and Jerry Copeland*. Tyler, Tex.: privately published, 1996.

Copeland, Kenneth W. *Primer of Beliefs for United Methodists*. Nashville, Tenn.: Tidings, 1959.

———. "A New Year's Wish For My Church." *The Methodist Woman*, n.d.

———. "Essentials to Effective Evangelism." *The Upper Room Pulpit* (February 1952).

———. "Jurisdictional Conference." *Travis Park News*, 21 June 1960.

———. "The Pastoral Prayer." *The New Christian Advocate* (Feb. 1957).

The Corsican, vol. xv, yearbook of Corsicana High School, Corsicana, Tex.: 1930.

"Dr. Copeland's Messages Bringing Wide Response" editorial. *San Antonio Express*, 19 May 1959.

Dunnam, Spurgeon M., III. "Dr. Copeland: Man of Persuasion." *The Texas Methodist* (March 1970).

Fancher, Carroll. "Ministerial Meanderings . . . " *First Methodist Visitor*, Bryan, Tex.: (16 Aug. 1973).

Haase, Lois, "Profiling the Life of a Bishop's Wife." *San Antonio Express-News*, 21 Oct. 1979.

High, Stanley, "Methodism's Pink Fringe." *Reader's Digest* (Feb. 1950).

BIBLIOGRAPHY

McAnally, Tom. "Bishop with a Pastor's Heart." *The Methodist Woman* (March 1966).

McCulloh, Gerald O., ed. *My Call to Preach*. Nashville, Tenn.: Methodist Evangelistic Materials, 1962.

Nail, Olin W. *The First One Hundred Years: The Southwest Texas Conference of the Methodist Church*. Austin, Tex.: Capital Printing Company, 1958.

Nail, Olin W., ed. *History of Texas Methodism 1900–1960*. Austin, Tex.: Capital Printing Company, 1961.

Robinson, Jessie Mae. *Milestones of Faith: Celebrating the African American Presence in the United Methodist Church 1968–1998*. Houston, Tex.: Office of Education and Teaching Ministries of the Texas Annual Conference, 1998.

Robinson, Richard Howard and Jessie Mae. *Historical Pictorial Souvenir Book, Methodist Bicentennial 1784–1984*. Houston, Tex.: Pha Green Printing Inc./Texas Annual Conference, 1984.

Short, Roy H. *History of the Council of Bishops of The United Methodist Church 1939–1979*. Nashville, Tenn.: Abingdon, 1980.

Spellmann, Norman W. *Growing a Soul: The Story of A. Frank Smith*. Dallas, Tex.: SMU Press, 1979.

Texas Conference Journal. Houston, Tex.: Texas Annual Conference, 1974.

Vernon, Walter N. *The Methodist Excitement in Texas*. Dallas, Tex.: United Methodist Historical Society, 1984.

Vernon, Walter N. *Methodism Moves Across North Texas*. Dallas, Tex.: The Historical Society, North Texas Conference of The Methodist Church, 1967.

Index

Page numbers in bold indicate entries in the insert located between pages 112 and 113.

235

INDEX

INDEX

INDEX

Methodist Board of Evangelism, 50, 72
Methodist Board of Missions, 88, 120
Methodist Board of Pensions, 120
Methodist Church, xi, 82
Methodist Committee on Family Life, 88
Methodist Episcopal Church, 9, 21, 22, 25,
Methodist Episcopal Church South, 2, 9, 21, 23, 25, 85
Methodist Federation for Social Action, 128
Methodist Hospital, Houston, Texas, 137
Methodist Protestant Church, viii, xi, 9, 21, 22, 24–25, 85, 124, 126
Methodist Student Movement, 97
Methodist-EUB union, 113, 115, 135
Mexia, Texas, 21
Midlothian, Oklahoma, 2
Milestones of Faith, 122, 123
Milhouse, Paul W., 82
Moore, Arthur J., 75
Moore, John M., 25, 75
Moore, Noah W., 115
Mouzon, Edwin D., 75
Mt. Vernon, Texas, 35
Muzorewa, Abel T., 132
My Call to Preach, 5, 71
My Creed for Peace, 102

Nail, Olin W., 21
Nebraska, xi, 27, 52, 77–104, 113, 117, 125
Nebraska Annual Conference, xii, 131
Nebraska Area News Edition of *Together* magazine, 81
Nebraska Conference Women's Society of Christian Service, 101
Nebraska Wesleyan University, 90, 95, 96, 97, 131, 132

Newman Methodist Church, Lincoln, Nebraska, 84
Norris, Alfred L., 120
North Texas Conference of the Methodist Church, 24, 26

Okinawa, 100
Oklahoma A&M (Oklahoma State University), 19, 38, 42, 46, 62
Oklahoma Area, 38, 49, 120
Oklahoma City University, 9, 40
Old Mutare High School, 132
Old Mutare Mission Farm, 133
Oral Roberts University, 214
Oxnam, G. Bromley, 55
Ozark Mountain region, 1

Pakistan, 100, 207
Perkins Chapel, 139
Perkins School of Theology, xv, 19, 66, 156
Perkins, J.J. "Joe," 28
Philippines, 91, 100
Pope, W. Kenneth, 73
Primer of Beliefs for Methodist Laymen, 71
Primer of Beliefs for United Methodists, 71

Quinton, Oklahoma, 9, 10

Randolph, W.B., 118, *I–14*, *I–15*
Reader's Digest, 55
Rhodesia, 132
Richardson, J. A., 22
Robinson, Jessie Mae, 123–24
Robinson, Richard H., 118, 123, *I–14*
Rohlfs, Claus, 139

Salem Headlight, 2
San Angelo, Texas, 13–14

INDEX

San Antonio Chamber of
Commerce, 113
San Antonio Council of
Churches, 69
San Antonio Express, 53–54
San Antonio Express-News, 90, 146
San Antonio Lions Club, 69
San Antonio, ix, 49-75, 146
Schweitzer, Albert, 167
Scotland Methodist Church,
Wichita Falls, Texas, 26
Second Vatican Council, xi, 81
Shamblin, J. Kenneth, 105, 120,
147–48
Shirra, Walter M. "Wally" Jr., 127
Short, Roy H., 25, 49, 89, 91
Singapore, 90
Slater, O. Eugene, 73, 143
Slocum, Texas, 12
Smith, A. Frank, 45, 58–59, 70,
73, 89, 92, *I–7*
Smith, Bess, 139
Smith, W. Angie, 27–28, 38, 45,
49, 70, 138–39, *I–9*
Solomon, Dan E., 75
South Central Jurisdictional
Conference 1948, 40, 73
South Central Jurisdiction of the
Methodist Church, 27, 72
South Central Jurisdictional
Conference of the Methodist
Church 1944, 38
South Central Jurisdictional
Conference of the Methodist
Church 1960, ix, 73, 78
South Central Jurisdictional
Conference of the Methodist
Church 1964, 81
South Central Jurisdictional
Conference of the United
Methodist Church 1972, 91
South Central Jurisdictional
Conference of the United
Methodist Church 1968, 115
South Central Jurisdictional
Conference of the United
Methodist Church, 1980, 146

South Central Jurisdictional
Conference of the United
Methodist Church, 1984, 146
Southeast Asia, 90
Southern Methodist University,
16–17, 19, 40, 72, 105, 139, 156
Southern Rhodesia, 131
Southwest Texas Annual
Conference, 63, 73, 124, 146
Southwest Texas Methodist
Hospital, 145
Southwestern University, 53, 70
Sparks, Oklahoma, 5–6
Spellman, Norman W., 58
Spirit of St. Louis, 9
Springer, Franklin, 42
Spurgeon, Charles Haddon, 178
St. Luke's Methodist Church,
Oklahoma City, 42
St. Paul's Methodist Church,
Omaha, Nebraska, 87
Stafford, Thomas, 127
Stamps-Baxter Quartet, 31
Stillwater, Oklahoma, 39–48, 62
Stowe, W. McFerrin, 122, 139
Straughn, James H., 24–25, *I–11*
Streeter, Emmett S., 84

Taiwan, ix, 90, 100
Tehuacana, Texas, 11
Temple, C. Chappell, 122–23
Texas Alcohol and Narcotics
Education, Inc., 69
Texas Annual Conference of the
United Methodist Church
1974, 120
Texas Annual Conference of the
United Methodist Church, 115,
117, 119, 120, 133
Texas Conference Journal 1974,
105, 147
Texas Conference of the
Methodist Protestant Church,
10, 19, 21–23, 25
Texas Conference, ix, x, 121, 124,
132, 140, 142

INDEX

Texas State Historical
   Commission, 60
Thailand, 100
The Methodist Excitement in Texas,
   23
The Methodist Woman, 93, 106
The New Christian Advocate, 71
The South Central Jurisdiction
   1939–1972: A Brief History and
   an Interpretation, 73
The Texas Methodist, 129
The Upper Room Pulpit, 71, 107
Thielicke, Helmut, 175
Thomas Page A., xv, 105
Titus, Phylemon, 118, **I–15**
Travis Park Methodist Church,
   45–47, 49–50, 53, 55, 57, 60,
   62, 69, 73, 143, **I–5**
Travis Park News, 46, 73
Trinity University, 66, 69, 72
Tyler Morning Telegraph, 121

Ulsan, Korea, 100, 101
Union Methodist Church,
   Omaha, Nebraska, 84
United Methodist Board of
   Discipleship, 49, 128, 147
United Methodist Church, xi, 82
United Methodist Commission
   on Archives and History, 60
United Methodist Commission
   on Religion and Race, 119, 135
United Methodist Commission
   on the Status and Role of
   Women, 135
United Methodist Foundation for
   Evangelism, x, 146
United Methodist General
   Conference 1968, 113, 129,
   134, 149
United Methodist General
   Conference 1972, 127, 134–35
United Methodist General
   Conference 1980, 146
United Methodist Women, 142
University of Nebraska, 132

University Park United Methodist
   Church, Dallas, Texas, 202

Vernon, Walter, 23
Vietnam, xi, 95, 103–4, 128, 210,
   221
Vincent, John J., 158

Walton, Aubrey G., 73
Warman, John B., 74
Warwick, Oklahoma, 7
Wellston, Oklahoma, 9
Wesley, Charles, 89, **I-13**
Wesley, John, viii, 1, 46, 88, 193,
   I-12, I-13
Wesley's Chapel, 100, **I-12**
Westminster College, 11, 19, 24
White River Annual Conference, 2
Whittier, John Greenleaf, 157
Wichita Falls, Texas, 26–28
Wilcox, W. H., 45
Wiley College, 121, 146
Wilford, Boone L., 2
Williams, Charles W., 87, 125
Williams, Kelly, 143, 144
Williams, Vester, 2
Williamson, R. V., 165
Windsor Village United Methodist
   Church, Houston, 120
Wischer, Irene Cox, 51, 52, 53
Woman's Society of Christian
   Service, 157
Women's Christian Temperance
   Union, 34
World Methodist Conference
   1966, 99
World Methodist Council, 137
World War I, 2
World War II, viii, 34
Wortham, Texas, 10

Young, John W., 127

Zimbabwe, 131

240